MW01076992

COLLECTED WORKS OF RENÉ GUÉNON

MISCELLANEA

RENÉ GUÉNON

MISCELLANEA

Translators
H.D. Fohr, C. Bethell
P. Moore, H. Schiff

SOPHIA PERENNIS
HILLSDALE NY

Originally published
in French as *Mélanges*

First English Edition 2003
Second Impression 2004

Series editor: James R. Wetmore

For information, address:
Sophia Perennis, P.O. Box 611
Hillsdale NY 12529
www.sophiaperennis.com

Library of Congress Cataloging-in-Publication Data

Guénon, René
[Mélanges. English]
Miscellanea / René Guénon ; translated by Henry D. Fohr,
Cecil Bethell, Hubert Schiff, Patrick Moore

p. cm. — (Collected Works of René Guénon)
Includes bibliographical references and index.
ISBN 0 900588 55 1 (pbk: alk. paper)
ISBN 0 900588 56 x (cloth: alk. paper)
1. Religion. 2. Philosophy I. Title
BL50.G8413 2001
200—dc21 2001000902

CONTENTS

PART THREE: SOME MODERN ERRORS

EDITORIAL NOTE

The past century has witnessed an erosion of earlier cultural values as well as a blurring of the distinctive characteristics of the world's traditional civilizations, giving rise to philosophic and moral relativism, multiculturalism, and dangerous fundamentalist reactions. As early as the 1920s, the French metaphysician René Guénon (1886–1951) had diagnosed these tendencies and presented what he believed to be the only possible reconciliation of the legitimate, although apparently conflicting, demands of outward religious forms, 'exoterisms', with their essential core, 'esoterism'. His works are characterized by a foundational critique of the modern world coupled with a call for intellectual reform; a renewed examination of metaphysics, the traditional sciences, and symbolism, with special reference to the ultimate unanimity of all spiritual traditions; and finally, a call to the work of spiritual realization. Despite their wide influence, translation of Guénon's works into English has so far been piecemeal. The *Sophia Perennis* edition is intended to fill the urgent need to present them in a more authoritative and systematic form. A complete list of Guénon's works, given in the order of their original publication in French, follows this note.

What is here presented as a 'miscellany' of essays would in the case of most other writers on metaphysical subjects be considered a major work, both in breadth and depth. Some claim that René Guénon's views never 'developed', that his knowledge of metaphysics was innate, as primordial and unchangeable as truth itself. Though clearly an exaggeration—for example, A.K. Coomaraswamy and Marco Pallis led Guénon to considerably revise his views Buddhism—there is still a remarkable degree of truth to this claim. Information must be acquired, and in the process erroneous notions will be corrected; yet the capacity for intellective insight is not an acquisition, but a gift; it is developed not by adding something, but by removing a veil.

Some of the essays in the present volume could be considered Guénon's 'juvenalia', yet the unerring instinct for metaphysical truth is already there, fully formed, along with the first stirrings of the author's lifelong preoccupation with initiatic spirituality, the cosmological sciences, and the errors of modernity; there is no real incompatibility of outlook here between the Guénon of 1909 and the Guénon of 1950. Far from being a mere collection of fugitive writings, *Miscellanea* is an important work in its own right, worthy of its own unique place in the Guénonian corpus.

Guénon often uses words or expressions set off in 'scare quotes'. To avoid clutter, single quotation marks have been used throughout. As for transliterations, Guénon was more concerned with phonetic fidelity than academic usage. The system adopted here reflects the views of scholars familiar both with the languages and Guénon's writings. Brackets indicate editorial insertions, or, within citations, Guénon's additions. Wherever possible, references have been updated, and English editions substituted.

The present translation is based on the work of Henry Fohr, Patrick Moore, Cecil Bethell, and Hubert Schiff. The text was checked for accuracy and further revised by Marie Hansen. For help with selected chapters and proofreading thanks go to John Riess, John Champoux, Michael Allen, Allan Dewar, and John Ahmed Herlihy. A special debt of thanks is owed to Cecil Bethell, who revised and proofread the text at several stages and provided the index. Cover design by Michael Buchino and Gray Henry, based on a drawing of band design details from Grecian pottery of the sixth century BC, by Guénon's friend and collaborator Ananda K. Coomaraswamy.

THE WORKS OF RENÉ GUÉNON

Introduction to the Study of the Hindu Doctrines (1921)

Theosophy: History of a Pseudo-Religion (1921)

The Spiritist Fallacy (1923)

East and West (1924)

Man and His Becoming according to the Vedānta (1925)

The Esoterism of Dante (1925)

The Crisis of the Modern World (1927)

The King of the World (1927)

Spiritual Authority and Temporal Power (1929)

The Symbolism of the Cross (1931)

The Multiple States of the Being (1932)

The Reign of Quantity and the Signs of the Times (1945)

Perspectives on Initiation (1946)

The Great Triad (1946)

The Metaphysical Principles of the Infinitesimal Calculus (1946)

Initiation and Spiritual Realization (1952)

Insights into Christian Esoterism (1954)

Symbols of Sacred Science (1962)

Studies in Freemasonry and the Compagnonnage (1964)

Studies in Hinduism (1966)

Traditional Forms and Cosmic Cycles (1970)

Insights into Islamic Esoterism and Taoism (1973)

Reviews (1973)

Miscellanea (1976)

FOREWORD

IN ORDER TO MAKE THEM AVAILABLE in a book and to spare readers extended searches in back issues of journals long out of print, we have gathered together under the title of *Miscellanea* various articles by René Guénon and by 'Palingenius', his pseudonym during the time of *La Gnose*, a journal he founded in 1909. These articles have been divided into three categories: 'Metaphysics and Cosmology', 'Traditional Arts and Sciences', and 'Some Modern Errors'. From the first chapter of part one, 'The Demiurge', which we believe is the first text he ever submitted for publication, in 1909 at the age of twenty-three, to 'Profane Science in Light of Traditional Doctrines', of April–May 1950, more than forty years elapsed. In this period of nearly a half-century, it cannot be said that Guénon's intellectual positions changed much, especially with regard to his criticisms of the modern world.

With regard to the theoretical exposition of traditional doctrine, it is likely that he would have written 'The Demiurge' differently at certain points, although without changing its deeper meaning, for his metaphysical point of view always remained the same.

'Monotheism and Angelology' (1946), explains the polytheistic fallacy as a degeneration of traditional forms resulting from the incomprehension of the true relationships between diverse attributes and the Supreme Principle. Here Guénon repeats an argument of Sri Shankarāchārya in his commentary on the *Māṇḍūkya Upanishad*, but under a form more accessible to Westerners. The reader will note that, even in 'The Demiurge', Shankarian citations are already numerous.

'Spirit and Intellect' (1947) explains that the meaning of words is a function of the different orders of reality to which they are applied. The Intellect, or *Buddhi*, is of an essentially supra-individual nature because it is nothing other that the very expression of *Ātmā* in manifestation. If one therefore takes the word 'Spirit' in the sense of 'Intellect', it must be understood as a universal principle, the first production of *Prakriti*.

Contrary to some opinions, the subject of 'The Eternal Ideas' (1947) must not be considered as mere virtualities with regard to manifested beings, of which they are the principial 'archetypes', for

> there can be nothing virtual in the Principle but, quite the contrary, the permanent actuality of all things in an 'eternal present', an actuality which precisely constitutes the only real foundation of all existence.

To view things differently is equivalent to 'cutting the roots of plants'. 'It is not our reality in the Principle that is ever virtual, but rather the consciousness we are able to have of this while we are in manifestation.'

Chapter six, 'Know Thyself', is Guénon's translation and revision of an article in Arabic that he published in 1931 in the journal *El-Ma'rifa*. Let us recall that Guénon left for Cairo in March 1930, but that his 'connection' to the *Taṣawwuf* went back to 1912.

'On Mathematical Notation' and 'On the Production of Numbers' were written during the time of *La Gnose*, in 1910. The first was taken up again and developed in *The Metaphysical Principles of the Infinitesimal Calculus* (1946) in the collection 'Tradition'. The second, written in the summer of 1930, was a sequel to 'The Demiurge'. One can detect there the influence of Pythagorism and the Kabbalah (see *Traditional Forms and Cosmic Cycles*, pt. 3).

'Initiation and the Crafts' is a later article, appearing in *Le Voile d'Isis* in April 1934. Here the author explains why initiation became necessary in the measure that humanity receded from the 'primordial state'. As in 'The Arts & their Traditional Conception', Guénon here explains the reasons for the degeneration of the arts and crafts due to the 'fall' or descending trajectory of the present cycle. He nonetheless points out the possibility of an initiation into the 'lesser mysteries' based upon the craft of building which still exists validly in the West (cf. on this subject *Perspectives on Initiation*).

It is unfortunate that Guénon did not have the time to complete 'The Conditions of Corporeal Existence', begun in January and February 1912, in the last two issues of *La Gnose*. Thus, despite the fact that the text reproduced here deals only with *Ākashā* and *Vāyu*, while the other three elements—Fire, Water, Earth (*Tejas, Ap, Prithvī*)—are not treated, we thought that what was written would sufficiently interest the public for whom it was intended and that it was appropriate to include it with the other chapters of *Miscellanea*.

'Gnosis & the Spiritist Schools' brings us back to our starting-point, that is, to the period of 'The Demiurge', November 1909. This is a definitive assertion of his position, for, writes Guénon

> a universal Principle cannot be inferred from particular facts.... It is only within ourselves that we can find the principles of knowledge, and never in outward things.

Part Three brings together critiques aimed at the so-called spiritualist schools, that is, the occultists, Theosophists, and spiritualists, critiques which would be taken up again and developed in *The Spiritist Fallacy* and *Theosophism: History of a Pseudo-Religion* several years later.

Finally, the last chapter, 'Profane Science in Light of Traditional Doctrines', dated April 1950, reaffirms the same positions as those from the time of *La Gnose*, but this time *vis-a-vis* scientism:

> It is the profane point of view as such that is illegitimate, and this point of view consists essentially in considering things without a link to any transcendent principle and as if they were independent of every principle.... Modern science has no right to be considered as true knowledge since, even if it should happen to state things that are true, its manner of presenting them is nonetheless illegitimate, and it is in any case unable to give the reason for their truth which can only lie in their dependence on principles.... The practical applications that can result from this science ... are completely independent of the value of the science as such.... Scientists themselves readily recognize that they make use of forces the nature of which is completely unknown to them. This ignorance no doubt accounts for much of the danger that these applications too often present....

Today, after a half-century, it would be difficult to deny the justice of Guénon's last warnings.

This will certainly not prevent the destiny of the human cycle from being accomplished, but perhaps it will allow some a better understanding of the age in which we live and the never-ending pertinence of the works of the man whom Sri Ramana Maharshi called 'the great Sufi'.

ROGER MARIDOT

METAPHYSICS AND COSMOLOGY

1

THE DEMIURGE

THERE are a certain number of problems which have constantly preoccupied men, but perhaps none has ever seemed so insoluble as that of the origin of evil, a problem which most philosophers, and especially theologians, encounter as an insurmountable obstacle: *Si Deus est, unde Malum? Si non est, unde Bonum?* [If God is, whence Evil? If He is not, whence the Good?] In fact, this dilemma is insoluble for those who consider Creation as the direct work of God, and who, consequently, have to make him equally responsible for good and evil. One may well say that this responsibility is to a certain extent attenuated by the creatures' freedom; but if the creatures can choose between good and evil, this means that both already exist, at least in principle; and if they are prone to sometimes deciding in favor of evil rather than being always inclined toward good, this is because they are imperfect. How then can God, if he is perfect, create imperfect beings?

Obviously the perfect cannot engender the imperfect, for, if that were possible, the perfect would have to contain within itself the imperfect in the principial state, and then it would no longer be the perfect. Therefore the imperfect cannot proceed from the perfect by way of emanation, and can only result from creation *ex nihilo*. But how can one accept that something can come from nothing, or, in other words, that anything can exist without having a principle? Moreover, to admit creation *ex nihilo* would be to acknowledge *ipso facto* the final annihilation of created beings, for what has a beginning must also have an end; and nothing is more illogical than to speak of immortality under such an hypothesis. But creation thus understood is an absurdity, for it is contrary to the principle of causality, which it is impossible for any reasonable man to deny sincerely; and we can say with Lucretius: *Ex nihilo nihil, ad nihilum nil posse reverti* [Nothing comes from nothing; nothing can revert to nothing].

There can be nothing that does not have a principle; but what is this principle? and is there in actual fact only one Principle of all things? If the entire universe is considered, it is certainly obvious that it contains all things, for all parts are contained within the whole. On the other hand, the whole is necessarily unlimited, for if it had a limit, whatever exceeded that limit would not be included within the whole, and this supposition is absurd. That which has no limit can be called the Infinite, and since it contains everything, this Infinite is the principle of all things. Moreover, the Infinite is necessarily one, for two Infinites that are not identical would exclude one another. Hence there is only one unique Principle of all things—and this Principle is the Perfect, for the Infinite can only be such if it is the Perfect.

Thus, the Perfect is the supreme Principle, the primal Cause; it contains all things potentially and it has produced all things. But then, since there is only one unique Principle, what becomes of all the opposites that are usually considered in the universe: Being and Non-Being, spirit and matter, good and evil? Hence we find ourselves again in the presence of the same question we posed at the outset; and we can now formulate the question in a more general way: how has unity been able to produce duality?

Certain people have found it necessary to admit two distinct principles opposed to each other; but this hypothesis is ruled out by what we said previously. In fact, these two principles cannot both be infinite, for they would then exclude each other, or else they would be identical. If only one was infinite, it would be the principle of the other. Finally, if both were finite they would not be true principles, because to say that what is finite can exist by itself amounts to saying that something can come from nothing—since whatever is finite has a beginning, logically, if not chronologically. Consequently, in the latter case, since both are finite they must proceed from a common principle, which is infinite, and so we are brought back to the consideration of one unique Principle. Furthermore, many doctrines usually considered dualistic are so only in appearance. In

Manicheism as well as in the Zoroastrian religion, dualism was only a purely exoteric doctrine, concealing the true esoteric doctrine of Unity: Ormuzd and Ahriman are both engendered by Zervane-Akerene, and must merge in him at the end of time.

Hence duality is necessarily produced by unity, since it cannot exist by itself, but how can it be produced? In order to understand this, we must first of all consider duality under its least particularized aspect, which is the opposition between Being and Non-Being. Moreover, since both are necessarily contained within the total Perfection, it is obvious in the first place that this opposition can only be apparent. It would thus be better to speak only of distinction; but of what does this distinction consist? Does it exist as a reality independent from us, or is it merely the result of our way of viewing things?

If by Non-Being one understands only pure nothingness, it is useless to speak about it, for what can be said about that which is nothing? But if Non-Being is considered as the possibility of being, then this is completely different. In this sense, Being is the manifestation of Non-Being and is contained in a potential state within Non-Being. The relationship of Non-Being to Being is then that of the non-manifested to the manifested, and it can be said that the non-manifested is superior to the manifested (of which it is the principle) since it contains potentially the whole of the manifested, plus that which is not, has never been, and never will be manifested. At the same time it can be seen that here it is impossible to speak of a real distinction, since the manifested is contained principially within the non-manifested. However, we cannot conceive the non-manifested directly, but only through the manifested; this distinction therefore exists for us, but only for us.

If such is the case for duality under the aspect of the distinction between Being and Non-Being, the same holds true with greater reason for all other aspects of duality. From this it is already easy to see how illusory is the distinction between spirit and matter, a distinction on which, nevertheless, so many philosophical systems are built, especially in modern times, as if on an unshakable basis; if this distinction disappears, nothing is left of all these systems. Furthermore, we can point out in passing that duality cannot exist without the ternary, for if in differentiating itself the Supreme Principle gives rise to two elements (which moreover are only distinct insofar as we view them as such), these two elements, together with their common Principle, form a ternary, so that in reality it is the ternary, and not the binary, which is directly produced by the first differentiation of the primordial unity.

Let us now come back to the distinction of good and evil, which too is only a particular aspect of duality. When good and evil are opposed to each other, the good is usually seen to lie in Perfection, or, at a lower degree at least, as a tendency toward Perfection, so that evil is then nothing other than the imperfect. But how could the imperfect oppose the Perfect? We have seen that the Perfect is the Principle of all things and that, on the other hand, it cannot produce the imperfect, from which it follows that in reality the imperfect does not exist, or at least that it only exists as a constituent element of total Perfection; but then it cannot really be imperfect, and what we call imperfection is only relativity. Thus, what we call error is only relative truth, for all errors must be included within total Truth, or else the latter, being limited by something external to itself, would not be perfect, which amounts to saying that it would not be the Truth. Errors, or rather relative truths, are only fragments of the total Truth, so that it is fragmentation that produces relativity, and consequently could be said to be the cause of evil—if relativity is really synonymous with imperfection. But evil is such only if it is distinguished from the good?

If the perfect is called good, the relative is not really distinct from it, since it is contained within it principially. Therefore evil does not exist from the universal point of view. It will exist only if all things are considered in a fragmentary and analytical light, separating them from their common Principle, instead of viewing them as contained synthetically within this Principle, which is Perfection. Thus is the imperfect created; in distinguishing evil from good, both are created by this very distinction, for good and evil are such only when they are opposed to each other. If there is no evil, there is no longer any reason to speak of good in the ordinary sense of this word, but only of Perfection. It is thus the fatal delusion of dualism that realizes good and evil, and which, considering things from a particular point of view, substitutes multiplicity for unity, and thus encloses the beings who are under its spell within the sphere of confusion and division. This sphere is the Empire of the Demiurge.

II

What we have just said concerning the distinction of good and evil makes it possible to understand the symbol of the original Fall, at least insofar as such things can be expressed. The fragmentation of total Truth, or of the Word—for fundamentally they are the same thing—a fragmentation that produces relativity, is identical to the dismemberment of Adam Kadmon, whose separated fragments constitute protoplastic Adam, namely the first creator of forms. The cause of this segmentation is Nahash—egoism, or the desire for individual existence. Nahash is not a cause external to man but is within him, potentially at first, and becomes external to him only insofar as man himself exteriorizes it. This instinct of separativity, which by its very nature provokes division, induces man to taste the fruit of the Tree of Knowledge of Good and Evil, that is, to create the very distinction of good and evil. Thus man's eyes open, for what was internal to him has become external as a result of the separation that has arisen between beings; from now on beings assume forms which limit and define their individual existence, and so man was the first maker of forms. But henceforth he too is subject to the conditions of this individual existence and he also assumes a form, or, according to the biblical expression, a tunic of skin. He is enclosed within the sphere of good and evil, within the Empire of the Demiurge.

This essay, very abridged and incomplete though it is, makes it evident that the Demiurge is not a power external to man. In principle he is merely man's will, inasmuch as this will realizes the distinction between good and evil. But then man, limited as an individual being by this will which is his very own, regards it as something external to himself, and thus it becomes distinct from him. Furthermore, as it opposes the efforts he makes to escape from the sphere in which he has enclosed himself, he views it as a hostile power and calls it Satan or the Adversary. Let us note, moreover, that this

Adversary, whom we ourselves created and whom we create moment by moment—for this should not be considered as having taken place at a given time—is not evil in itself, but is merely the whole of everything that is adverse to us.

From a more general point of view, once the Demiurge has become a separate power and is considered as such, he is the Prince of this World mentioned in Saint John's Gospel. Here again, strictly speaking, he is neither good nor bad, or rather he is both, since he contains within himself both good and evil. His sphere is regarded as the lower world, as opposed to the upper world or principial Universe from which it has been separated, but it should be carefully noted that this separation is never absolutely real. It is real only insofar as we realize it, for this lower world is contained potentially within the principial Universe, and it is obvious that no part can really depart from the Whole. This is what keeps the fall from going on indefinitely; however, this is only a purely symbolic expression and the depth of the fall simply measures the degree to which the separation is realized. With this reservation in mind, the Demiurge is opposed to Adam Kadmon or principial Mankind, manifestation of the Word, but only as a reflection, for he is not an emanation and does not exist by himself. This is what is represented by the two old men of the Zohar, and also by the two opposed triangles of the Seal of Solomon.

We are thus led to consider the Demiurge as a dark and inverted reflection of Being, for in reality he cannot be anything else. So he is not a being; but according to what we said earlier, he can be considered as the community of the beings to the extent that they are distinct, or if one prefer, insofar as they are endowed with individual existence. We are separate beings insofar as we ourselves create the distinction, which only exists insofar as we create it. As creators of this distinction, we are elements of the Demiurge; and to the extent that we are distinct beings, we belong to the sphere of this same Demiurge, which is what we call Creation.

All elements of Creation, namely the creatures, are therefore contained within the Demiurge himself, and he cannot in fact draw them out of anything but himself, since creation *ex nihilo* is impossible. As Creator, the Demiurge first produces division, from which he is not really distinct, since he exists only inasmuch as division itself exists. And then, as division is the source of individual existence, which in turn is defined by form, the Demiurge should be considered as the form-maker, and as such he is identical to protoplastic Adam, as we have seen. One can also say that the Demiurge creates matter, understood in the sense of the primordial chaos that is the common reservoir of all forms. Then he organizes this chaotic and dark matter, in which confusion reigns, bringing forth from it the multiple forms the totality of which constitutes Creation.

Now, must one say that this Creation is imperfect? Certainly, it cannot be regarded as perfect; however, from a universal point of view, it is merely one of the constituent elements of total Perfection. It is imperfect only when considered analytically as separated from its Principle, and it is moreover in the same extent that it is the sphere of the Demiurge. But if the imperfect is merely an element of the Perfect, then it is not really imperfect, and consequently the Demiurge and his sphere do not really exist from the universal point of view, any more than does the distinction between good and evil. From the same point of view it also follows that matter does not exist: material appearance is only an illusion. However, one should not conclude from this that beings with a material appearance do not exist, for this would amount to succumbing to another illusion, that of an exaggerated and poorly understood idealism.

If matter does not exist, the distinction between spirit and matter thereby disappears. Everything must in reality be spirit, but spirit understood in a completely different sense from that attributed to it by most modern philosophers. In fact, while opposing spirit to matter, they still do not consider spirit as independent of all form, and one may then wonder in what way it is differentiated from matter. If it is said that spirit is unextended whereas matter is extended, how then can that which is unextended assume a form? Moreover, why should one want to define spirit? Whether by thought or otherwise, one always attempts to define it by means of a form, and then it is no longer spirit. In reality, the universal spirit is Being, and not such or such a being in particular, but the Principle of all beings, and thus it contains them all. This is why everything is spirit.

When man reaches real knowledge of this truth, he identifies himself and all things with the universal Spirit. Then all distinctions vanish for him, so that he contemplates everything as being within himself, and no longer as external, for illusion vanishes before Truth like a shadow before the sun. By this very knowledge, then, man is freed from the bonds of matter and individual existence; he is no longer subject to the domination of the Prince of this World, he no longer belongs to the Empire of the Demiurge.

III

From the preceding it follows that beginning with his earthly existence man can free himself from the sphere of the Demiurge, or the hylic world, and that this emancipation is achieved through gnosis, that is, through full knowledge. Let us further point out that this knowledge has nothing to do with analytical science, and does not imply it in any way. It is too widespread an illusion nowadays to believe that total synthesis can only be attained through analysis. On the contrary, ordinary science is quite relative, and, limited to the hylic world as it is, does not exist any more than this world, from the universal point of view.

Moreover, we must also point out that the different worlds—or, according to a generally accepted expression, the various planes of the universe—are not places or regions, but modalities of existence or states of being. This enables one to understand how a man living on the earth might in reality no longer belong to the hylic world, but to the psychic or even to the pneumatic world. It is this that constitutes the second birth; however, strictly speaking, this birth is only a birth into the psychic world, through which man becomes conscious on two planes but without yet reaching the pneumatic world, that is, without identifying himself with the universal Spirit. This last result is only obtained by the one who fully possesses the triple knowledge, by which he is forever liberated from mortal births; this is what is being expressed when it is said that only pneumatics are saved. The state of the psychics is, in short, only a transient state; it is that of the being that is already prepared to receive the Light, but that does not yet perceive it, that is not yet aware of the one and immutable Truth.

When we speak of mortal births, we mean the modifications of a being, its passage through multiple and changing forms. There is nothing here which resembles the doctrine of reincarnation, such as it is accepted by the spiritists and Theosophists, a doctrine which we might some day have the opportunity to explain.[1] The pneumatic is freed from mortal births, that is to say he is liberated from form, hence from the demiurgic world. He is no longer subject to change, and, consequently, is actionless; we shall come back to this point later. The psychic, on the contrary, does not pass beyond the World of Formation, which is symbolically designated as the first heaven or the Sphere of the Moon. From there he comes back to the terrestrial world, which does not in fact mean that he will actually take a new body on earth, but simply that he will need to assume new forms, whatever they may be, before obtaining Liberation.

What we have just said illustrates the agreement—we could even say the real identity, despite certain differences of expression—of the gnostic doctrine with the Eastern doctrines, particularly with the *Vedānta*, the most orthodox of all the metaphysical systems based on Brāhmanism. This is why we can complete what we have said about the various states of the being by borrowing a few quotations from *Self-Knowledge* [*Ātma-Bodha*] by Shankarāchārya:

> There is no other way of obtaining full and final Liberation than through Knowledge; it is the sole means which loosens the bonds of passion; without Knowledge, Beatitude cannot be obtained. Action, not being opposed to ignorance, cannot cast it away; but Knowledge dispels ignorance, as light dispels darkness.

Ignorance here means the state of a being shrouded in the darkness of the hylic world, attached to the illusory appearance of matter and to individual distinctions. Through knowledge, which is not within the sphere of action but superior to it, all these illusions vanish, as we said above.

1. Guénon came back to the question of reincarnation in *The Spiritist Fallacy* and *Theosophy: History of a Pseudo-Religion*. ED.

> When ignorance born of earthly affections is cast away, Spirit shines from the distance by Its own splendor in an undivided state, just as the Sun sheds its light when the cloud is dispersed.

But before reaching this state, the being goes through an intermediate stage corresponding to the psychic world. Then it no longer believes itself to be the material body but the individual soul, for all distinction has not vanished for it, since it has not yet departed the sphere of the Demiurge.

> Imagining that he is the individual soul, man becomes frightened like a person mistaking a piece of rope for a snake. But his fear is dispelled by the perception that he is not the soul, but the universal Spirit.

The one who has become aware of the two manifested worlds, namely the hylic (the totality of gross or material manifestations) and the psychic (the totality of subtle manifestations), is twice born, *dvija.* But the one who is aware of the unmanifested universe or the formless world—that is, the pneumatic world—and who has achieved the identification of himself with the universal Spirit, *Ātmā*, he alone can be called *yogi*, that is to say united with the universal Spirit.

> The Yogi, whose intellect is perfect, contemplates all things as abiding in himself and thus, through the eye of Knowledge, he perceives that everything is Spirit.

Let us note in passing that the hylic world is likened to the waking state, the psychic world to the dream state, and the pneumatic world to deep sleep. In this connection, we should recall that the unmanifested is superior to the manifested, since it is its principle. According to the gnostic doctrine there is nothing beyond the pneumatic Universe but the Pleroma, which can be viewed as constituted by the totality of attributes of the Divinity. This is not a fourth world, but is the universal Spirit itself, the Supreme Principle of the three worlds, neither manifested nor unmanifested, indefinable, inconceivable, and incomprehensible.

The *yogi* or pneumatic, for they are fundamentally the same thing, perceives himself no longer as a gross or subtle form, but as a formless being. Hence he identifies himself with the universal Spirit, a state which Shankarāchārya describes as follows:

> He is Brahma beyond whose possession there is nothing to be possessed; beyond whose happiness once enjoyed there is no happiness which could be desired; and beyond whose knowledge once obtained there is no knowledge that could be obtained.
> He is Brahma who having once seen, no other object is contemplated; with whom once identified, no birth is experienced; whom once perceived, there is nothing more to be perceived.
> He is Brahma who is spread everywhere, all-pervading: in mid-space, in what is above and what is below; the true, the living, the happy, non-dual, indivisible, eternal and one.
> He is Brahma without size, unextended, uncreated, incorruptible, figureless, without qualities or character.
> He is Brahma by whom all things are illuminated, whose light makes the Sun and all luminous bodies shine, but who is not made manifest by their light.
> He himself permeates his own eternal essence and he contemplates the whole World appearing as being Brahma.
> Brahma does not resemble the World, and apart from Brahma there is nothing; whatever seems to exist apart from him is an illusion.
> Of all that is seen, of all that is heard, nothing exists other than Brahma; and through knowledge of the principle, Brahma is contemplated as the real Being, living, happy, non-dual.
> The eye of Knowledge contemplates the true, living, happy, all-pervading Being; but the eye of ignorance does not discover It, does not catch sight of It, just as a blind man does not see the light.
> When the Sun of spiritual Knowledge arises in the sky of the heart, It casts away darkness, pervades everything, embraces everything and illuminates everything.

Let us point out that the Brahma here in question is the superior Brahma. It should be carefully distinguished from the inferior *Brahmā*, for the latter is none other than the Demiurge, regarded as a reflection of the Being. For the Yogi there is only the superior Brahma, who contains all things and apart from whom there is nothing; for him, the Demiurge and his work of division no longer exist.

> The one who has accomplished the pilgrimage of his own spirit, a pilgrimage in which there is nothing connected to the situation, the place, or the time, which is everywhere, in which neither heat nor cold are experienced, which bestows eternal happiness and freedom from all sorrow, that one is actionless; he knows everything and obtains eternal Beatitude.

IV

After having characterized the three worlds and the corresponding states of the being, and having indicated as far as possible what being is liberated from the demiurgic domination, we must once again return to the question of the distinction between good and evil, in order to draw a few consequences from the preceding exposition.

First of all, one might be tempted to say that if the distinction between good and evil is sheer illusion, if it does not exist in reality, the same should hold true for morality, for moral standards are obviously based on this distinction, since they essentially imply it. But this would be going too far; morality does exist, but only to the same extent as the distinction between good and evil, that is, for anything that belongs to the sphere of the Demiurge; from the universal point of view, it no longer has any raison d'être. Morality, in fact, can apply only to action; now action implies change, which is only possible in the formal or manifested order. The formless world is immutable, superior to change, and therefore also to action; and this is why the being no longer belonging to the Empire of the Demiurge is actionless.

All this shows that one should take great care never to confound the various planes of the universe, for what is said about one could be untrue for another. So, morality necessarily exists on the social plane, which is essentially the field of action, but it can no longer be in question when the metaphysical or universal plane is considered, since thenceforth there is no more action.

Having established this point, we should mention that the being that is superior to action nevertheless possesses the fullness of activity, but it is a potential activity, hence an activity that does not act. This being is not motionless, as might be wrongly said, but immutable, that is to say superior to change; indeed, it is identified with Being which is ever identical to itself, according to the biblical formula 'Being is Being'. This must be compared with the Taoist doctrine, according to which the Activity of Heaven is non-acting. The sage, in whom the Activity of Heaven is reflected, observes non-action; nevertheless, the sage, whom we designated as the pneumatic or the *yogi*, can give the appearance of action, just as the moon appears to move when clouds pass over it; but the wind that blows away the clouds has no influence on the moon. Similarly, the agitation of the demiurgic world has no effect on the pneumatic; in this connection, we can again quote what Shankarāchārya says:

> The Yogi, having crossed the sea of passions, is united with Tranquility and rejoices in the Spirit.
> Having renounced these pleasures that are born of external and perishable objects, and enjoying spiritual delights, he is calm and serene like the lamp placed inside a jar, and rejoices in his own essence.
> During his residence in the body, he is not affected by its properties, just as the firmament is not affected by what is floating within its bosom; knowing all, he remains unaffected by contingencies.

By this we can understand the real meaning of the word *Nirvāna*, to which so many wrong interpretations have been given. This word literally signifies extinction of the breath or of agitation, therefore the state of a being no longer subject to any agitation, ever free from form. At least in the West, it is a very widespread error to believe that when there is no more form, there is nothing, whereas in reality it is form that is nothing and the formless that is everything. Thus, far from being annihilation, as certain philosophers have contended, *Nirvāna* is on the contrary the plenitude of Being.

From all that has been said till now, one could draw the conclusion that one should not act; but this would again be inaccurate, if not in principle, at least in the application that one would like to draw from it. In fact, action is the condition of individual beings belonging to the Empire of the Demiurge. The pneumatic or the sage is really actionless, but as long as he resides in a body he gives the appearance of action. Externally, he is in all respects like other men, but he knows this is only an illusory appearance, and this is enough to set him truly free from action, since it is through knowledge that Deliverance is obtained. By the very fact that he is free from action, he is no longer subject to suffering, for suffering is merely the result of effort, hence of action, and it is this that constitutes what we call imperfection, although there is nothing imperfect in reality.

Obviously action cannot exist for the one who contemplates within himself all things as existing within the universal Spirit, without any distinction of individual objects, as is expressed in these words from the Vedas: 'Objects differ merely in designation, accident and name just as earthly utensils receive various names, although they are only different forms of earth.' The earth, principle of all these forms, is itself formless, but contains them all potentially; such also is the universal Spirit.

Action implies change, namely the unceasing destruction of forms which disappear in order to be replaced by others. These are the modifications that we call birth and death, the multiple changes of state which any being that has not yet attained liberation or the final transformation (transformation taken here in its etymological sense, that of passing beyond form) must traverse. Attachment to individual things, or to essentially transient and perishable forms, is characteristic of ignorance. Forms are nothing for the being liberated from form, and this is why it is not affected by the properties of the latter, even during its residence in the body.

> Thus he moves about free as the wind, for his movements are not impeded by the passions.
> When forms are destroyed, the Yogi and all beings enter the all-pervading essence.
> He is devoid of qualities and actionless; imperishable and without volition; happy, immutable, faceless; eternally free and pure.

> He is like ether which is spread everywhere and pervades simultaneously both the inside and the outside of things; he is incorruptible, imperishable; he is the same in all things, pure, undisturbed, formless, immutable.
> He is the great Brahma who is eternal, pure, free, one, unceasingly happy, non-dual, existing, perceiving and endless.

Such is the state attained by a being through spiritual knowledge; thus is it forever free from all the conditions of individual existence, and thus liberated from the Empire of the Demiurge.

Not appealing!
God is Infinte potentiality
– always evolving, eternally
unfolding

2

MONOTHEISM AND ANGELOLOGY

WHAT WE SAID earlier makes it possible to understand the nature of the error that tends to give rise to polytheism: this latter, which in short is but the most extreme case of 'association',[1] consists of admitting a plurality of totally independent principles, whereas in reality these are and can be only more or less secondary aspects of the supreme Principle. It is obvious that this can only be the result of a failure to understand precisely those traditional truths that refer to the divine aspects or attributes. Such a lack of understanding is always possible among isolated individuals, whatever their number, but its generalization, which corresponds to the state of extreme degeneration of a traditional form about to disappear, has no doubt been far more uncommon in fact than is usually believed. In any case, no tradition whatsoever could ever be polytheist in itself; it is a reversal of all normal order to suppose, as do the 'evolutionist' views of most moderns, a polytheism at the origin rather than to see therein only the simple deviation that it is in reality. All genuine tradition is essentially monotheistic; more specifically, it affirms above all the oneness of the supreme Principle,[2] from which

1. There is 'association' as soon as it is admitted that anything whatsoever outside of the Principle possesses its own proper existence; naturally there are many degrees from this to polytheism properly so called.

2. When it is truly a question of the supreme Principle, one should in all strictness speak of 'non-duality', since unity, which is an immediate consequence thereof, is merely situated on the level of Being. Although this distinction is of the greatest metaphysical importance, it has no effect on what we have just said here; just as we can generalize the sense of the term 'monotheism', we can also and correlatively just speak of the unity of the Principle.

everything is derived and on which it entirely depends, and it is this affirmation that, especially in the guise in which it is clothed in the traditions having a religious form, constitutes monotheism in the strict sense of the word; but, having given this explanation in order to avoid any possible confusion of points of view, we can ultimately extend the meaning of the term monotheism so as to apply it to every affirmation of principial unity. On the other hand, when we say that monotheism is therefore necessarily at the origin, it goes without saying that this is in no way related to the hypothesis of a so-called 'primitive simplicity', which probably never existed.[3] Furthermore, to avoid any misunderstanding in this respect, it is enough to note that monotheism can include all the possible developments connected with the multiplicity of divine attributes, and also that angelology, which is closely related to the consideration of these attributes as we have already explained, plays an important role in the traditional forms where monotheism is affirmed most explicitly and rigorously. Thus no incompatibility exists here, and even the invocation of the angels is perfectly legitimate and normal from the strictest monotheistic point of view, provided they are considered solely as 'celestial intermediaries', that is to say, finally, as representing or expressing certain divine aspects within the order of supra-formal manifestation, according to what we have already explained.

In this connection we should also mention certain misuses of the so-called 'historical' point of view dear to many of our contemporaries, and particularly as regards the theory of 'borrowings' which we have already mentioned on various other occasions. Indeed, to give an example, we have quite often seen authors claim that the Hebrews did not know anything about angelology before the captivity in Babylon and that they simply borrowed it from the Chaldeans, while others maintain that all angelology, wherever encountered, invariably proceeds from Mazdaism. It is clear enough that similar assertions implicitly suppose that angelology belongs to the sphere

3. Cf. *The Reign of Quantity and the Signs of the Times*, chap. 11. — Moreover, it is very difficult to understand how some people can at the same time believe both in 'primitive simplicity' and in original polytheism, yet so it is. This is again a curious example of the innumerable contradictions of the modern mentality.

of mere 'ideas' in the modern and psychological sense of this word, or of baseless concepts, whereas for us—as for all those who share the traditional point of view—on the contrary it concerns knowledge of a certain order of reality. It is hard to imagine why such knowledge should have been 'borrowed' by one doctrine from another, whereas it is very easy to understand that it is inherent to one as well as the other, since both are expressions of one and the same truth. The same knowledge can and must be found everywhere; and when we speak here of equivalent knowledge, we mean knowledge that is basically the same, but presented and expressed in different ways in order to adapt to the special constitution of this or that traditional form.[4] In this sense, it could be said that angelology or its equivalent—whatever its particular designation—exists in all the traditions; it is hardly necessary to recall for instance that in the Hindu tradition, the *Devas* are the exact equivalent of the angels of the Judaic, Christian, and Islamic traditions. In all cases, what is in question can be defined as the part of a traditional doctrine that refers to supra-formal or supra-individual states of manifestation, either purely theoretically or in view of an actual realization of these states.[5] It is obvious that in itself this is something that does not have the slightest connection with any kind of polytheism, even if, as we have said, polytheism can only be the result of a lack of understanding of such matters, but when those who believe in the existence of polytheistic traditions speak of 'borrowings' such as those mentioned above, they seem to want to suggest thereby that angelology represents nothing but a 'contamination' of monotheism by polytheism! This would amount to saying that because idolatry can arise from the misunderstanding of certain symbols, symbolism itself is only a derivation of idolatry; the above case would be completely similar, and we think the comparison is more than enough to point out how absurd such a view is.

4. Previously we alluded to the links between angelology and the sacred languages of the different traditions. This is a characteristic example of what is here in question.

5. As an example of the first one could cite that part of Christian theology related to angels (and in a general way, moreover, exoterism can only take a theoretical point of view here), and as an example of the second, the 'practical Kabbalah' in the Hebrew tradition.

To conclude these remarks, which are meant to complete our preceding study, let us quote this passage from Jacob Boehme, who, with his characteristic terminology and somewhat obscure form, seems to us to express correctly the relationship of the angels to the divine aspects:

> The creation of the angels has a beginning, but the forces from which they were created never knew a beginning, but were present at the birth of the eternal beginning.... They are born of the revealed Word, out of the eternal, dark, fiery, and luminous nature, from desire for divine revelation, and have been turned into 'creatured' images [that is, fragmented into isolated creatures].[6]

And Boehme says elsewhere: 'Each angelic prince is a property come out of the voice of God, and he bears God's great name.'[7] A.K. Coomaraswamy, quoting this last sentence and comparing it with various texts about 'Gods' in the Greek as well as the Hindu tradition, adds these words, which fully accord with what we have written above:

> We hardly need say that such a multiplicity of Gods is not polytheism, for all are the angelic subjects of the Supreme Deity from whom they originate and in whom, as is so often recalled, they again become one.[8]

6. *Mysterium Magnum*, viii, 1.

7. *De Signatura Rerum*, xvi, 5. — On the subject of the first creation 'going out from the mouth of God,' cf. *Perspectives on Initiation*, chap. 47.

8. 'What is Civilization?', in Albert Schweitzer Festschrift [republished in *What is Civilisation?* (Great Barrington, MA: Lindisfarne Press, 1989)]. — In this connection, Coomaraswamy also mentions Philo's identification of the angels with the Platonic 'Ideas', that is, in short, the 'Eternal Reasons', contained in the divine understanding, or, according to the language of Christian theology, in the Word considered as the 'place of possibles'.

3

SPIRIT AND INTELLECT

It has been pointed out that, while it is often affirmed that the spirit is not other than *Ātmā*, there are nevertheless instances in which this same spirit seems to be identified only with *Buddhi*; is there not something contradictory here? It would not suffice to see in this a simple question of terminology, for if such were the case one could just as well go further and accept indiscriminately the many more or less vague and incorrect meanings commonly given to the word 'spirit', instead of carefully avoiding them, as we have always tried to do; and the only too evident inadequacy of Western languages regarding the expression of ideas of a metaphysical order is, to say the least, certainly no reason for not taking all the precautions necessary to avoid confusion. What justifies these two uses of the same word, let us state it at the outset, is the correspondence that exists between different 'levels' of reality, and that makes possible the transposition of certain terms from one of these levels to another.

The case in question is in short comparable to that of the word 'essence', which can also be applied in several different ways. Insofar as it is correlative to 'substance', it designates, from the point of view of universal manifestation, *Purusha* envisaged in relation to *Prakriti*; but it can be transposed beyond this duality,[1] and such is necessarily the case when one speaks of the 'Divine Essence', even if,

1. The use of the term *Purushottama* in the Hindu tradition implies precisely the same transposition in relation to that which *Purusha* designates in its most common sense.

as usually happens in the West, those who use this expression do not go beyond pure Being in their conception of the Divinity. Similarly, one can speak of the essence of a being as complementary to its substance, but one can also designate as essence that which constitutes the ultimate, immutable, and unconditioned reality of that being; and the reason for this is that the first is after all nothing other than the expression of the second in regard to manifestation. Now, if one says that the spirit of a being is the same as its essence, this can also be understood in both of these two senses, and from the point of view of absolute reality, spirit or essence obviously is not and cannot be anything other than *Ātmā*. Only, it must be noted that *Ātmā*, comprising all reality within itself principially, for that very reason cannot enter into correlation with anything whatsoever. Thus, as long as it is a question of the constitutive principles of a being in its conditioned states, what is considered spirit (as for example in the ternary 'spirit, soul, and body') can no longer be the unconditioned *Ātmā*, but only that which so to speak most directly represents it in manifestation. We would add that this is no longer even the essence correlative to substance, for although it is true that this latter must be considered in relation to manifestation, it is nevertheless not within manifestation itself; therefore, properly speaking it will only be the first and highest of all manifested principles, that is, *Buddhi*.

From the point of view of a state of manifestation such as the individual human state, it is therefore necessary to introduce what could be called a question of 'perspective'; thus, when we speak of the universal, distinguishing it from the individual, we must thereby understand not only the unmanifested, but also that which in manifestation itself is non-individual, that is, supra-formal manifestation, to which *Buddhi* essentially belongs. Similarly, with regard to the individuality as such, including as it does the entirety of the psychic and corporeal elements, we can only designate as spiritual the principles that are transcendent in relation to this individuality, which again is precisely the case with *Buddhi*, or the intellect. This is why we can say, as we often have, that for us pure intellectuality and spirituality are fundamentally synonymous; and furthermore the intellect itself can also be transposed as in the cases above, since it is generally considered quite acceptable to speak of the 'Divine Intellect'. In this connection, we will again note that although the *gunas* are inherent in *Prakriti*, only *sattva* can be considered as a spiritual tendency (or 'spiritualizing' tendency, if one prefers) because it is the tendency that orients the being toward the higher states. This, in short, is a consequence of the same 'perspective' that presents the supra-individual states as intermediary degrees between the human state and the unconditioned state, although between the latter and any conditioned state whatsoever, even the most elevated of all, there is really no common measure.

What must be emphasized most particularly is the essentially supra-individual nature of the pure intellect; moreover, only that which belongs to this order can truly be called 'transcendent', as this term normally can be applied only to what lies beyond the individual domain. The intellect is thus never individualized; this again corresponds to what, from the more particular point of view of the corporeal world, is expressed when it is said that whatever the appearances may be, the spirit is never really 'incarnated', which moreover is equally true of all the legitimate senses of the word 'spirit'.[2] It follows that the distinction existing between the spirit and elements of the individual order is much more profound than all those distinctions which can be established among these elements themselves, and notably between the psychic and corporeal elements, that is, between those which belong respectively to subtle and gross manifestation, both of which are after all only modalities of formal manifestation.[3]

But this is still not all: not only does *Buddhi* constitute the link between all the states of manifestation insofar as it is the first production of *Prakriti*, but from another perspective and considered

2. It could even be said that generally this marks the clearest and the most important distinction between these senses and the illegitimate meanings which are too often attributed to this same word.

3. This is also why in all strictness a man cannot speak of 'his spirit' as he speaks of 'his soul' or 'his body', the possessive implying that it is a question of an element belonging properly to the individual order. In the ternary division of the elements of the being, the individual as such is composed of soul and body, while the spirit (without which it could not exist in any manner) is transcendent in relation to it.

from the principial point of view, it appears as the luminous ray emanating directly from the spiritual Sun, which is *Ātmā* itself. It can therefore be said that *Buddhi* is also the first manifestation of *Ātmā*,[4] even though it must be clearly understood that *Ātmā* itself always remains unmanifest, not being affected or modified by any contingency.[5] Now, light is essentially one, and is not of a different nature in the sun and in the sun's rays, which latter, from the point of view of the sun itself, are distinguishable from the former only in an illusory mode (although this distinction is nonetheless real for the eye which perceives these rays, and which here represents the being situated within manifestation).[6] By reason of this essential 'connaturality', *Buddhi* is ultimately none other than the very expression of *Ātmā* in the manifested order. This luminous ray which links all the states together is also represented symbolically as the 'breath' by which they subsist—which, let us note, is in strict conformity with the etymological sense of the words designating spirit, whether this be the Latin *spiritus* or the Greek *pneuma*; and as we have already explained on other occasions, it is properly the *sūtrātmā*, which amounts to saying that in reality it is *Ātmā* itself, or, more precisely, the appearance which *Ātmā* takes from the moment that, instead of considering only the supreme Principle (which would then be represented as the sun containing in itself all the rays in an 'indistinguished' state), we also consider the manifested states. Moreover, this appearance, which seems to give to the ray an existence distinct from its source, is such only from the point of view of the beings within these manifested states, for it is evident that the 'exteriority' of the manifested states in relation to the Principle can only be altogether illusory.

The immediate conclusion to be drawn from these considerations is that as long as the being is not only in the human state, but

4. Cf. *The Great Triad*, chap. 8, n13.

5. According to the Upanishadic formula, it is 'That by which everything is manifested, which is not itself manifested by anything.'

6. Light is the traditional symbol of the very nature of the spirit; we have remarked elsewhere that one also encounters, in this regard, the expressions 'spiritual light' and 'intelligible light', as if they were in some way synonymous, which, again, obviously implies an assimilation between the spirit and intellect.

in any manifested state whatsoever, either individual or supra-individual, there can be for it no effective difference between the spirit and the intellect, nor, consequently, between spirituality and true intellectuality. In other words, in order to arrive at the supreme and final goal, there is no other path for this being but the very ray by which it is linked to the spiritual Sun; whatever the apparent diversity of paths at the point of departure, sooner or later they must all be united in this one 'axial' path; and when the being has followed this path to the end, it 'will enter into its own Self', which it has been outside of only illusorily, because this 'Self'—called analogically spirit, essence, or whatever name one wishes—is identical to absolute reality in which everything is contained, that is, supreme and unconditioned *Ātmā*.

4

THE ETERNAL IDEAS

WITH regard to the identification of spirit with intellect, we noted in the preceding chapter that no one hesitates to speak of the 'Divine Intellect', which obviously implies a transposition of this term beyond the domain of manifestation; but this point deserves further attention, for ultimately it is here that the very basis for this identification is to be found. Let us immediately note that here again one can place oneself at different levels, according to whether one stops at the consideration of Being alone, or whether one goes beyond Being; but in any case it is obvious that when theologians consider the Divine Intellect or the Word as the 'place of possibles', they have in view only possibilities of manifestation, which as such are included in Being. The transposition that allows the shift from Being to the Supreme Principle no longer pertains to the domain of theology, but solely to that of pure metaphysics.

One might wonder whether this conception of the Divine Intellect is identical to Plato's 'intelligible world', or, in other words, whether the 'ideas' understood in the Platonic sense are the same as those contained eternally in the Word. In both cases, it is clearly a question of the 'archetypes' of manifested beings; however, at least at first glance, the 'intelligible world' might seem to correspond to the supra-formal order of manifestation rather than to that of pure Being, or, according to Hindu terminology, it would be identical to *Buddhi* envisaged in the Universal sense rather than to *Ātmā*, even were *Ātmā* taken in a sense restricted to the consideration of Being alone. Both points of view are of course perfectly legitimate,[1] but, if

1. It might be of some interest to mention that the 'idea' or 'archetype', envisaged within the order of the supra-formal manifestation, and with reference to

such is the case, then the Platonic 'ideas' cannot properly be called 'eternal', for this word cannot be applied to anything that belongs to manifestation, even manifestation at its highest degree and closest to the Principle, whereas the 'ideas' contained in the Word are necessarily eternal, as is the Word, since whatever is of the principial order is absolutely permanent and immutable and admits of no kind of succession.[2] Notwithstanding this, it appears to us quite probable that the passage from one of these points of view to the other must have remained possible for Plato himself, as in reality it still remains. We will not dwell further on this, however, preferring to leave to others the task of examining this question more closely, its interest being after all more historical than doctrinal.

What is rather strange is that some people seem to consider the eternal ideas as mere 'virtualities' in relation to the manifested beings of which they are the principial 'archetypes'. Here is a delusion that is doubtless due to the common distinction between the 'possible' and the 'real', a distinction which, as we explained elsewhere, could not have the least value from the metaphysical point of view.[3] This delusion is all the more grave in that it leads to a real contradiction, and it is difficult to understand how it can go unnoticed. In fact, there can be nothing virtual within the Principle but, on the contrary, only the permanent actuality of all things in an 'eternal present', and it is this very actuality that constitutes the sole foundation of all existence. Still, there are those who push the misunderstanding so far that they seem to regard eternal ideas merely as kinds of images (which, let us note in passing, implies a further contradiction in wanting to introduce something of a formal nature even into the Principle), images that have no more real a connection

each being, basically corresponds, despite the different mode of expression, to the Catholic concept of the 'guardian angel'.

2. We do not differentiate here between the domain of Being and that which is beyond, for it is obvious that the possibilities of manifestation, whether considered especially as contained within Being or as contained along with all others within Total Possibility, do not really differ. The sole difference lies simply in the point of view or the 'level' from which things are viewed, according to whether or not one considers the relation of these possibilities with manifestation itself.

3. See *The Multiple States of the Being*, chap. 2.

with the beings themselves than would their reflected image in a mirror. This is strictly speaking a complete reversal of the relationship of the Principle with manifestation, which is too obvious to require further explanation. The truth is indeed very far from all such erroneous conceptions: the idea in question here is the very principle of the being; it is that which gives it all its reality and without which it would be only nothingness pure and simple. To maintain the contrary amounts to severing all links between the manifested being and the Principle, and if at the same time a real existence is attributed to the being, this existence cannot but be independent of the Principle, whether or not one wishes it, so that, as we said on another occasion,[4] one inevitably ends up in the error of 'association'. From the moment one recognizes that the existence of manifested beings in all their positive reality can only be a 'participation' in principial Being, there cannot be the slightest doubt about this matter. If one were to admit this 'participation' simultaneously with the so-called 'virtuality' of the eternal ideas, one would face yet another contradiction. What is in fact virtual is not our reality within the Principle, but only the awareness we may have of it as manifested beings, which is obviously something quite different; and it is only through metaphysical realization that this awareness of our true being, which is beyond and above all 'becoming', can become effective, that is, actualized into the awareness, not of something that might pass as it were from 'potency' to 'act', but rather an awareness of that which we really are principially and eternally, and this in the most absolutely real sense possible.

Now, to relate what we have just said about eternal ideas to the manifested intellect, one must naturally turn once again to the doctrine of the *sūtrātmā*, regardless of the form under which it is expressed, for the various symbolisms traditionally used in this respect are basically perfectly equivalent. Thus, to return to the representation we used earlier, it can be said that the Divine Intellect is the spiritual Sun, while the manifested intellect is one of its rays;[5]

4. See 'The Roots of Plants', in *Symbols of Sacred Science*, chap. 62. [See also chapter two of the present book. Ed.]

5. Moreover, this ray will be single insofar as *Buddhi* is envisaged at the Universal level (it is then the 'one foot of the sun' of which the Hindu tradition also

and there can be no more discontinuity between the Principle and manifestation than there is between the sun and its rays.[6] It is thus by the intellect that every being in all its states of manifestation is directly attached to the Principle, and this is because the Principle, insofar as it eternally contains the 'truth' of all beings, is itself none other than the Divine Intellect.[7]

---

speaks), but it will seemingly be multiplied indefinitely in relation to particular beings (as the *sushumnā* ray by which each being, in whatever state it is situated, is permanently linked to the spiritual Sun).

ular beings (as the *sushumna* ray by which each being, in whatever state it is situated, is permanently linked to the spiritual Sun).

6. These are the rays which, according to the symbolism that we explained elsewhere, realize manifestation through 'measuring' it by their actual extension from the sun (see *The Reign of Quantity and the Signs of the Times*, chap. 3).

7. In the terms of the Islamic tradition, *al-ḥaqīqah*, or the 'truth' of every being whatsoever, lies in the Divine Principle inasmuch as this Principle is itself *al-Ḥaqq* or the 'Truth' in the absolute sense.

5

SILENCE AND SOLITUDE

IN EVERY TRIBE without exception among the North American Indians, there exists, in addition to various kinds of collective rites, the practice of a solitary and silent worship, which is regarded as what is most profound and of the highest order.[1] To some degree, collective rites always have, in fact, something relatively external about them; we say 'to some degree' because in this as in every other tradition it is of course necessary to differentiate between rites that may be called exoteric, that is, those in which any and all may participate, and the initiatic rites. Moreover, it is quite clear that, far from excluding these rites or opposing them in any way, the worship here in question is merely superimposed on them as something of another order as it were; and there is even every reason to think that to be truly effective and to produce actual results, initiation is implied as a necessary prerequisite.[2]

1. This information is taken mainly from Paul Coze's work *The Thunderbird*, from which we also draw our quotations. The author shows a remarkable sympathy for the Indians and their tradition, and the only necessary reservation is that he seems rather strongly influenced by 'metapsychist' conceptions, which obviously affect some of his interpretations and in particular sometimes lead him to a certain confusion between the psychic and the spiritual. However, there is no room for such considerations in the matter that we are dealing with here.

2. It goes without saying that here, as always, we mean initiation in its true sense, not in that of the ethnologists, who use this word incorrectly to designate rites of admission to the tribe. One should take great care in making a clear distinction between these two things, both of which in fact exist among the Indians.

This worship is sometimes spoken of as 'prayer', but this is obviously inaccurate, for there is no petition of any kind; besides, prayers such as are generally expressed in ritual chants can only be addressed to the various divine manifestations,[3] and we will see that in reality what is here under consideration is something completely different. It would certainly be much more appropriate to speak of 'incantation', in the sense in which we have defined it elsewhere,[4] and it could also be spoken of as an 'invocation', in a sense exactly comparable to that of *dhikr* in the Islamic tradition, as long as it is made clear that it is essentially a silent and wholly interior 'invocation'.[5] Here is what Charles Eastman[6] writes in this connection: 'The worship of the Great Mystery was silent, solitary, without inner complication; it was silent because all speech is necessarily weak and imperfect, also the souls of our ancestors reached God through silent worship. It was solitary because they thought that God is closer to us in solitude, and there was no priest to serve as mediator between man and the Creator.'[7] In truth, there can be no intermediaries in such a case, since this worship tends to establish a direct communication with the Supreme Principle, which is designated here as the 'Great Mystery'.

Not only is it solely in and through silence that this communication can be obtained—for the 'Great Mystery' is beyond any form or expression—but silence itself 'is the Great Mystery'. How can this

3. In the Indian tradition, these divine manifestations seem usually to be distributed according to a quaternary division, in accordance with a cosmological symbolism which applies simultaneously to both the macrocosmic and the microcosmic points of view.

4. See *Perspectives on Initiation*, chap. 24.

5. In this connection, it is not without interest that certain Islamic *ṭuruq*, notably the *Naqshbandī*, also practice silent *dhikr*.

6. Charles Eastman, quoted by Paul Coze, was born a Sioux and seems to have retained a clear awareness of his own tradition despite a 'white' education. We have moreover good reason to believe that in reality such a case is far from being as exceptional as one might think if one stops at certain wholly external appearances.

7. The last word, only employed here as a result of habitual usage in European languages, is certainly not exact if one wants to get to the heart of the matter, for in reality 'God the Creator' can only be placed among the manifested aspects of the Divine.

assertion be properly understood? First of all, one may recall in this connection that the true 'mystery' is essentially and exclusively the inexpressible, which can obviously be represented only by silence.[8] Furthermore, since the 'Great Mystery' is the unmanifested, silence itself, which is precisely a state of non-manifestation, is thus like a participation in or conformity to the nature of the Supreme Principle. Moreover, silence, correlated to the Principle, is so to speak the unuttered Word; this is why 'sacred silence is the voice of the Great Spirit', insofar as the latter is identified with the Principle itself.[9] This voice, which corresponds to the principial modality of sound which the Hindu tradition calls *para* or unmanifested,[10] is the response to the call of a being at worship: call and response, alike silent, are an aspiration and an illumination that are both purely interior.

For this to be true, silence must in reality be something more than the mere absence of word or speech, even if they are in a purely mental form. In fact, for the Indians, silence is essentially 'the perfect balance of the three parts of the being,' that is, of what is known in Western terminology as spirit, soul, and body, for the whole being, in all its constituent elements, has to participate in the worship in order to obtain a fully valid result. The necessity for this condition of equilibrium is easy to understand, for within manifestation itself equilibrium is like the image or reflection of the principial indistinction of the unmanifested, an indistinction also well represented by silence, so that there is no cause to wonder at the assimilation that has thus been established between silence and balance.[11]

As for solitude, let us first of all point out that its association with silence is in a way normal and even necessary, and that whoever

8. See *Perspectives on Initiation*, chap. 17.

9. The reason for this reservation is that in certain cases the expression 'Great Spirit', or what one translates as such, seems also to be the particular designation of one of the divine manifestations.

10. See *Perspectives on Initiation*, chap. 47

11. There is hardly need to recall that the principial non-distinction in question here has nothing in common with what can also be designated by the same word in a lower sense, that is, the pure undifferentiated potentiality of the *materia prima*.

establishes perfect silence within himself is thereby, even in the presence of other beings, necessarily isolated from them. Moreover, silence and solitude are both implied in the meaning of the Sanskrit term *mauna*, which, in the Hindu tradition, is no doubt what applies most exactly to the state currently under consideration.[12] Multiplicity, being inherent to manifestation, and increasing as one descends to its lower degrees, necessarily removes one from the unmanifested. Also, the being that wishes to communicate with the Principle must first of all establish unity within itself to the degree possible by harmonizing and balancing all its elements; and at the same time it must isolate itself from all external multiplicity. The unification thus realized, even if still only relative in most cases, is nonetheless a certain conformity to the 'non-duality' of the Principle, in accordance with the present possibilities of the being. In the highest sense, isolation has the meaning of the Sanskrit term *kaivalya*, which simultaneously expresses the notions of perfection and of totality, and in its full significance even designates the absolute and unconditioned state, that of the being that has reached final Deliverance.

At a much lower degree than this, one still belonging only to the preliminary phases of realization, one notes the following: wherever dispersion necessarily exists, solitude, inasmuch as it opposes multiplicity and coincides with a certain unity, is essentially concentration; and indeed one is well aware of the importance accorded concentration by all the traditional doctrines without exception, as means and indispensable condition for any realization. It seems of little use to emphasize this point further, but there is yet another consequence to which we wish to draw attention in closing: the method in question, by opposing every dispersion of the being's powers, excludes the separate and more or less disorderly development of one or another of its elements, particularly that of the psychic elements cultivated for their own sake as it were, a development that is always contrary to the harmony and equilibrium of the whole. According to Paul Coze, for the Indians 'it seems that in

12. Cf. *Man and His becoming according to Vedānta*, chap. 23.

order to develop *orenda*,[13] the intermediary between the material and the spiritual, one must first of all dominate matter and tend toward the divine.' This amounts to saying that they consider it legitimate to approach the psychic domain only 'from above', since results of the psychic order are obtained only in a very secondary way and 'by way of addition' so to speak, which is in fact the sole means of avoiding the dangers; and let us add that this is assuredly as far removed from common 'magic' as can be, contrary to what has all too often been attributed to such results by profane and superficial observers, no doubt because they themselves do not have the least notion of what true spirituality can be.

13. This word belongs specifically to the Iroquoian language, but it has become customary in European works to use it generally in place of all other terms bearing the same meaning that can be found among the various Indian peoples. It designates the different modes of the psychic and vital force. It is therefore almost the exact equivalent of *prāna* in the Hindu tradition and *k'i* in the Far-Eastern tradition.

6

'KNOW THYSELF'

THE SAYING 'Know Thyself' is frequently cited, but its exact meaning is very often lost sight of. As for the prevailing confusion over this saying, two questions may be posed: the first concerns its origin, and the second its real meaning and raison d'être. Certain readers would like to believe that these two questions are entirely distinct and unrelated, but on reflection and after careful examination it becomes quite clear that they are in fact very closely connected.

If we ask students of Greek philosophy who is the man who first uttered these words of wisdom, most of them will not hesitate to reply that it was Socrates, although some of them attempt to link them to Plato and others to Pythagoras. From these contradictory views and divergences of opinion we may rightfully conclude that none of these philosophers is the author of this phrase and that one should not seek its origin with them.

This opinion seems permissible to us, as it will to the reader once he knows that two of these philosophers, Pythagoras and Socrates, left no writings. As for Plato, whatever his philosophical competence might be, we are even unable to distinguish his own words from those of his master Socrates. Most of Socrates' doctrine is known to us only through Plato, who, as is well known, garnered some of the knowledge displayed in his *Dialogues* from the teachings of Pythagoras. It is thus extremely difficult to determine what comes from each of the three philosophers: what is attributed to Plato is often attributed to Socrates as well, and, among the theories brought forward, some predate both of them and come from the school of Pythagoras, or from Pythagoras himself.

In truth, the origin of the saying in question goes back much further than the three philosophers here mentioned; better yet, it is older than the history of philosophy, even passing beyond the domain of philosophy. It is said that this saying was inscribed over the door of the Temple of Apollo at Delphi. It was adopted by Socrates, and likewise by other philosophers, as one of the principles of their teaching, despite the difference existing between these various teachings and the ends pursued by their authors. It is probable moreover that Pythagoras had employed this expression long before Socrates. By this saying these philosophers intended to show that their teaching was not strictly personal, that it came from an older starting-point, from a more elevated point of view rejoining the very source of its original inspiration, which was spontaneous and divine. We note that in this these philosophers differed greatly from modern philosophers, who expend all their efforts in expressing things anew so as to present them as the expression of their own thought, and to pose as the sole authors of their opinions, as if truth could be the property of one man.

We shall now see why the ancient philosophers wished to attach their teaching to this saying, or to a similar one, and why it can be said that this maxim is of an order superior to all philosophy. To reply to the second part of this question, then, let us say that the answer is contained in the original and etymological meaning of the word 'philosophy', which is said to have been used for the first time by Pythagoras. The word 'philosophy' properly expresses the fact of loving *Sophia*, or wisdom, the aspiration toward it or the disposition required for acquiring it. This word has always been used to signify a preparation for this acquisition of wisdom, and especially such studies as could help the *philosophos*, or the man who felt some inclination toward wisdom, to become a *sophos*—that is, a sage. So, just as the means cannot be taken as an end, the love of wisdom cannot constitute wisdom itself. And since wisdom in itself is identical with true inner knowledge, it can be said that philosophical knowledge is only a superficial and outward knowledge. Hence it does not have an independent value in itself or by itself; it constitutes only a first degree on the path of the superior and veritable knowledge which is wisdom.

Those who have studied the ancient philosophers know well that these latter had two kinds of teaching, one exoteric and the other esoteric. What had been written down belonged only to the first. As for the second, it is impossible for us to know its precise nature, for on the one hand it was reserved for a few, and on the other hand it had a secret character. There would have been no reason for these two characteristics had there not existed something higher than mere philosophy. One may at least surmise that this esoteric teaching had a close and direct connection with wisdom, and that it did not only appeal to reason or to logic, as is the case with philosophy, which for this reason has been called rational knowledge—the philosophers of antiquity maintained that rational knowledge, that is, philosophy, is not the highest degree of knowledge, is not wisdom.

Is it possible that wisdom could be taught in the same way that exterior knowledge is taught, through speech or through books? This is in fact impossible, as we shall shortly see. But what we can already affirm now is that philosophical preparation was not enough, even as preparation, for it concerns only the limited faculty of reason, whereas wisdom concerns the reality of the whole being. Hence there exists a preparation for wisdom which is higher than philosophy, which no longer addresses itself to reason, but to the soul and to the spirit, and which we may call inner preparation; and it appears to have been the characteristic of the highest levels of the school of Pythagoras. Its influence extended through the school of Plato right up to the Neoplatonism of the Alexandrian school, where it clearly appears anew, as well as among the Neo-Pythagoreans of the same period.

If words were still made use of in this inner preparation, they could now only be taken as symbols for the purpose of focusing inner contemplation. Through this preparation, man was led to certain states which enabled him to go beyond the rational knowledge that he had attained earlier, and since all of this lay beyond the level of reason, it was also beyond philosophy, for the name 'philosophy' is in fact always used to designate something pertaining to reason alone. It is nonetheless surprising that the moderns should have come to consider philosophy, thus defined, as if it were complete in itself, thus forgetting what is higher and superior.

Esoteric teaching had been known in the lands of the East before spreading to Greece, where it received the name of 'mysteries'. The first philosophers, Pythagoras in particular, had linked their teaching to it, considering it as no more than a new expression of ancient ideas. There were several kinds of mysteries, of diverse origin. Those which inspired Pythagoras and Plato were connected with the cult of Apollo. The 'mysteries' always had a reserved and secret character—the word 'mystery' itself has the etymological meaning of 'total silence'—since they were in connection with things that could not be expressed in words, but could only be taught by a way of silence. But the moderns, knowing of no method other than one implying the use of words, and which we may call the method of exoteric teaching, for this reason falsely believed that these 'mysteries' conveyed no teaching at all. We can affirm that this silent teaching made use of figures, symbols, and other means the purpose of which was to lead man to certain interior states that would allow him gradually to attain real knowledge or wisdom. This was the essential and final purpose of all the 'mysteries' and of similar things found elsewhere.

As for the 'mysteries' specially connected with the cult of Apollo and with Apollo himself, it must be remembered that this latter was the god of the sun and of light—light in its spiritual sense being the source whence all knowledge springs forth and all the sciences and the arts derive. It is said that the rites of Apollo came from the north, and this refers to a very ancient tradition also found in sacred books like the Hindu *Veda* and the Persian *Avesta*. This northern origin was affirmed even more specially for Delphi, which was known as a universal spiritual center; and in its temple was a stone called *omphalos*, which symbolized the center of the world.

It is thought that the story of Pythagoras and even the name of Pythagoras have a certain link with the rites of Apollo. The latter was called *Pythios*, and it is said that Pytho was the original name of Delphi. The woman who received inspiration from the gods in the temple was called Pythia; the name of Pythagoras therefore signified 'the guide of Pythia', which was applied to Apollo himself. It is also said that it was the Pythia who had declared Socrates to be the wisest of men. From this it appears that Socrates had a link with the spiritual center of Delphi, as did Pythagoras himself.

Let us add that although all the sciences were attributed to Apollo, this was more particularly so for geometry and medicine. In the Pythagorean school, geometry and all the branches of mathematics were foremost in the preparation for higher knowledge. With regard to this knowledge itself, these sciences were not then set aside, but on the contrary remained in use as symbols of spiritual truth. Plato also considered geometry an indispensable preparation for every other teaching and had these words inscribed over the entrance of his school: 'Let no one enter who is not a geometrician.' The meaning of these words can be understood when they are linked to another of Plato's expressions, 'God always geometrizes', if we add that in speaking of a geometer God Plato was again alluding to Apollo. One should thus not be astonished that the philosophers of antiquity made use of the saying inscribed over the entrance to the temple of Delphi, for we now know what links bound them to the rites and to the symbolism of Apollo.

From all of this we can easily understand the real meaning of the saying under consideration, as well as the error of the moderns on this subject. This error arises from the fact that they have viewed the phrase as a simple saying of a philosopher, whose thought they always assume to be comparable to their own. But in reality ancient thought differed profoundly from modern thought. Thus many people impute a psychological meaning to this phrase, but what they call psychology consists only in the study of mental phenomena, which are no more than external modifications—and not the essence—of the being.

Others, particularly among those who attribute the phrase to Socrates, see in it a moral goal, the search for a law applicable to practical life. All these external interpretations, though not entirely false, do not justify the sacred character it had originally, and which implies a much more profound meaning than the one they would thus like to attribute to it. The saying signifies first and foremost that no exoteric teaching is capable of providing true knowledge, which man must find only within himself, for in fact no knowledge can be acquired except through a personal comprehension. Without this comprehension, no teaching can lead to an effective result, and the teaching that awakens no personal resonance in the one who receives it cannot give any kind of knowledge. This is why Plato says that 'everything that a man learns is already within him.' All the experiences, all the external things that surround him, are only an occasion to help him become aware of what is within himself. This awakening he calls *anamnesis*, which signifies 'recollection'.

If this is true for any kind of knowledge, it is all the more so for a more exalted and profound knowledge, and, when man advances toward this knowledge, all external and perceptible means become increasingly insufficient, until they finally become useless. Although they can assist to some degree in the approach to wisdom, they are powerless in actually attaining it. In India it is commonly said that the true *guru* or master is found within man himself and not in the external world, although in the beginning an external aid can be useful to prepare man to find within himself and by himself that which cannot be found elsewhere, and especially what is above the level of rational knowledge. In order to attain this, it is necessary to realize certain states which go ever deeper within the being, toward the center symbolized by the heart, and whither man's consciousness must be transferred in order to make him capable of attaining real knowledge. These states, which were realized in the ancient mysteries, are degrees on the path of this transposition from the mind to the heart.

As we said, in the temple of Delphi there was a stone called *omphalos*, which represented the center of the human being as well as the center of the world, in accordance with the correspondence existing between the macrocosm and the microcosm—that is to say, man—so that everything that is in the one is directly related to what is in the other. Avicenna said: 'You believe yourself to be nothingness, yet the world abides within you.' It is curious to note the widespread belief in antiquity that the *omphalos* had fallen from the sky, and an accurate idea of the sentiment of the Greeks regarding this stone can be had by saying it was somewhat similar to the sentiment Muslims feel with regard to the sacred black stone of the *Kaaba*.

The similarity which exists between the macrocosm and the microcosm is such that each is the image of the other, and the correspondence of the constitutive elements shows that man must first of all know himself so that he may then know all things, for in truth, he can find all things within himself. It is for this reason that certain sciences, especially those which were a part of ancient knowledge and are now almost unknown to our contemporaries, possess a double meaning. In their outward appearance, these sciences are related to the macrocosm, and can justly be considered from this point of view. But at the same time they have also a deeper meaning, which is related to man himself and to the inner path through which he can realize knowledge within himself, a realization which is none other than the realization of his own being. Aristotle has said: 'the being is all that it knows,' so much so that, where there is real knowledge, and not its appearance or its shadow, knowledge and being are one and the same thing.

The shadow, according to Plato, is knowledge through the senses and even rational knowledge which, although higher, has its source in the senses. As for real knowledge, it is above the level of reason, and its realization, or the realization of the being itself, is similar to the formation of the world, according to the correspondence which we have mentioned above. That is why certain sciences can describe it under the appearance of this formation; this double meaning was included in the ancient mysteries, as it is also to be met with in all kinds of teachings having the same goal among the peoples of the East. It seems that in the West, too, this teaching existed throughout the Middle Ages, even though today it may have completely disappeared to the point that most Westerners have no idea of its nature or even of its existence.

From all that has been said, we see that real knowledge is not based on the path of reason, but on the spirit and the whole being, for it is none other than the realization of this being in all its states, which is the culmination of knowledge and the attainment of supreme wisdom. In reality, what belongs to the soul, and even to the spirit, represents only degrees on the path toward the intimate essence that is the true self; this self can be found only when the being has reached its own center, all its powers being united and concentrated as in a single point in which all things appear to it, since they are contained in this point as in their first and unique principle; thus the being is able to know everything as in itself and of itself, as the totality of existence in the oneness of its own essence.

It is easy to see how far this is from psychology in the modern sense of the word, and that it goes even further than a truer and more profound knowledge of the soul, which can only be the first step on this path. It is important to note that the meaning of the Arabic word *nafs* should not be limited here to the soul, for this word is found in the Arabic translation of the saying in question, while its Greek equivalent *psyche* does not appear in the original. *Nafs* should therefore not be taken in its usual sense, for it is certain that it has another much higher significance, which makes it similar to the word essence, and which refers to the *Self* or to the *real being*; as proof of this, we can cite what has been said in a *ḥādith* that is like a complement of the Greek saying: 'He who knows himself, knows his Lord.'

When man knows himself in his deepest essence, that is, in the center of his being, then at the same time he knows his Lord. And knowing his Lord, he at the same time knows all things, which come from Him and return to Him. He knows all things in the supreme oneness of the Divine Principle, outside of which, according to the words of Muḥyi 'd-Dīn lbn al-'Arabī, 'there is absolutely nothing which exists,' for nothing can be outside of the Infinite.

7

ON THE PRODUCTION OF NUMBERS

'IN THE BEGINNING, before the origin of all things, was Unity,' say the loftiest of Western theogonies, which strive to reach Being beyond its ternary manifestation, not halting at the universal appearance of the Binary. But the theogonies of the East and Far East say: 'Before the beginning, before even the primordial Unity, was the Zero,' for they know that beyond Being there is Non-Being; that beyond the manifest there is the non-manifest, which is its principle; and that Non-Being is not nothingness, but on the contrary infinite Possibility, identical to the universal All, which is at the same time absolute Perfection and integral Truth.

According to the Kabbalah, the Absolute, in order to manifest itself, concentrates itself in an infinitely luminous point, leaving darkness around it. This light within the darkness, this point within limitless metaphysical extension, this nothing that is all in an all that is nothing, if one may so express it, is Being in the midst of Non-Being, active Perfection within passive Perfection. This luminous point is Unity, the affirmation of metaphysical Zero, here represented by unlimited extension; it is the image of infinite, universal Possibility. In order to serve as the center from which, like so many rays, the indefinite manifestations of Being will emanate, Unity once affirmed is united to Zero, which contains it in principle, that is, to the state of non-manifestation. Here the Decad already appears in potentiality, and it will be the perfect number, the complete development of the primordial Unity.

Total Possibility is at the same time universal Passivity, for it contains all particular possibilities, certain of which will be manifested, passing from potentiality to actuality under the action of Unity-Being. Each manifestation is a radius of the circumference that represents total manifestation; and this circumference, the points of which are indefinite in number, is again Zero in relation to its center, which is Unity. But the circle was not laid out in the Abyss of Non-Being, and it only marks the limit of manifestation, of the domain of Being within the heart of Non-Being; it is therefore Zero realized, and, through the totality of its manifestation following the indefinite circumference, Unity perfects its development into the Decad.

Moreover, with the affirmation of Unity even before all manifestation, if this Unity were opposed to Zero, which contains it in principle, the Binary would then appear within the Absolute itself, in the primary differentiation that leads to the distinction between Non-Being and Being. But in our study on the Demiurge we saw what this distinction is, and showed that Being, or active Perfection—*Khien*—is not really distinct from Non-Being, or passive Per-fection—*Khouen*—that this distinction, which is the point of departure for all manifestation, exists only insofar as we create it ourselves, since we can only conceive of Non-Being through Being, the non-manifest through the manifest; thus the differentiation between the Absolute within Being and the Absolute within Non-Being only expresses the manner in which we represent things to ourselves, and nothing more.

Viewing things in this light, one might be tempted to speak of the Absolute as the common principle of Being and Non-Being, of the manifest and the non-manifest, although in reality it should be identified with Non-Being, since the latter is the principle of Being, which in turn is itself the first principle of all manifestation. Thus if one should wish to consider the Binary here, one would immediately find oneself in the presence of the Ternary; but in order for such to be a true Ternary, that is, already a manifestation, the Absolute would have to be primordial Unity, and we have seen that Unity represents only Being, the affirmation of the Absolute. It is this Unity-Being that will be manifested in the indefinite multiplicity of numbers, the entirety of which it contains in potentiality, and which emanate from it like sub-multiples of itself; and all of these numbers are included within the Decad, realized through the course of the cycle of the total manifestation of Being. It is therefore the production of this Decad, starting from the primordial Unity, that we must now consider.

In a previous study, we saw that all the numbers can be considered to emanate from Unity in pairs; these pairs of inverse or complementary numbers, which may be regarded as symbolizing the syzygies of the Eons of the Pleroma, exist within Unity in the undifferentiated or non-manifest state:

$$1 = 1/2 \times 2 = 1/3 \times 3 = 1/4 \times 4 = 1/5 \times 5 = \ldots = 0 \times \infty$$

None of these groups, $1/n \times n$, is distinct from Unity, or from the other groups within Unity; they become so only when their constituent elements are considered separately; it is then that Duality is born, distinguishing one principle from the other, not in opposition, as is ordinarily—and wrongly—said, but as complementary principles; active and passive, positive and negative, masculine and feminine. But the two principles coexist within Unity, and their indivisible duality itself constitutes a secondary unity, a reflection of primordial Unity; thus, together with the Unity that contains them, the two complementary elements compose the Ternary, which is the first manifestation of Unity, for two, being the issue of one, cannot exist without three thereby existing as well:

$$1 + 2 = 3$$

And just as we can only conceive of Non-Being through Being, we can only conceive of Unity-Being through its ternary manifestation, the necessary and immediate consequence of the differentiation or polarization that our intellect creates within Unity. Whatever the aspect according to which this ternary manifestation is viewed, it is always an indissoluble Trinity, that is, a Tri-Unity, since the three terms are not really distinct, but are only the same Unity conceived as containing within itself the two poles through which it will produce all of manifestation.

This polarization is again found immediately within the Ternary itself, for if one considers its three terms to have an independent existence, one will thereby obtain the Senary number, implying a new ternary, which is the reflection of the first.

$$1 + 2 + 3 = 6$$

This second ternary has no real existence by itself; it is to the first what the Demiurge is to the emanative Logos, a tenebrous and inverted image, and in what follows we shall indeed see that the Senary is the number of Creation. For the moment let us content ourselves with saying that it is we who realize this number, as we distinguish the three terms of Tri-Unity, instead of envisaging principial Unity synthetically, independent of all distinction, that is, of all manifestation.

If the ternary is regarded as a manifestation of Unity, it will at the same time be necessary to consider Unity insofar as it is not manifested, and then Unity, joined to the Ternary, will produce the Quaternary, which can be represented here by the three vertices of a triangle, together with its center. One could also say that the Ternary, symbolized by a triangle of which the three vertices correspond to the first three numbers, necessarily presupposes the Quaternary, the first term of which, being unexpressed, would then be Zero, which indeed cannot be represented. Thus one could consider the first term within the Quaternary to be either Zero or primordial Unity. In the first instance, the second term will be Unity insofar as it is manifested, and the two others its double manifestation; in the second instance, on the contrary, these last two, the two complementary elements mentioned above, will logically have precedence over the fourth term (which is nothing other than their union), realizing between them an equilibrium in which principial Unity is reflected. Finally, if one considers the Ternary according to its lowest aspect, taking it to be formed from the two complementary elements and the equilibrating term, then the latter, as the union of the other two, will participate in both, such that one will be able to regard it as double; here again, the Ternary will immediately imply a Quaternary, which is its development.

Whatever manner in which one considers the Quaternary, one can say that it contains all numbers, for if its four terms are regarded as distinct, one will see that it contains the Decad:

$$1 + 2 + 3 + 4 = 10$$

This is why all the traditions say that one produced two, two produced three, three produced all numbers. The expansion of Unity in the Quaternary immediately realizes its total manifestation, which is the Decad.

The Quaternary is represented geometrically by the square, if the static state is considered, and by the cross, if the dynamic state is considered. When the cross turns about its center, it engenders the circle, which, together with its center, represents the Decad. This is what is called circling the square, and it is the geometric representation of the arithmetical fact set forth above; conversely, the Hermetic problem of squaring the circle will be represented by the division of the circle into four equal parts by means of two rectilinear diameters, and it will be expressed numerically by the preceding equation written in the opposite direction:

$$10 = 1 + 2 + 3 + 4$$

The Decad as formed by the set of the first four numbers, is what Pythagoras called the Tetraktys. In its entirety the symbol representing it had a ternary form, each of its exterior sides embracing four elements, and composed of ten elements in all. The figure is given, in a note, in the translation of the chapter on Pythagoras in the *Philosophumena.*

If the Ternary is the number that represents the first manifestation of principial Unity, then the Quaternity stands for its total expansion. This latter is symbolized by a cross of which the four branches are formed by two indefinite straight lines extending fully in each direction, and oriented along the four cardinal points of the indefinite, pleromatic circumference of Being, points the Kabbalah represents by the four letters of the Tetragrammaton, יהוה. The Quaternity is the number of the manifested Word, of Adam Kadmon, and one can say it is essentially the number of Emanation, for Emanation is the manifestation of the Word. From it, the other degrees of manifestation of Being are derived in logical succession, by the development of the numbers it contains within itself, the totality of which constitutes the Decad.

If the quaternary expansion of Unity is considered to be distinct from Unity itself, when it is added to Unity it produces the number five, and this again is symbolized by the cross with its four branches and center. Moreover, it will be the same for all new numbers whenever they are regarded as distinct from Unity, even if they cannot really be so, since they are only manifestations thereof; each of these numbers when added to primordial Unity, gives birth to the following number. Having pointed out this successive mode of production for numbers once and for all, we shall not return to it in what follows.

If the center of the cross is taken to be the starting-point for the four branches, it will represent the primordial Unity; if on the contrary it is only considered as their point of intersection, it will merely represent equilibrium, a reflection of Unity. This second point of view is marked Kabbalistically by the letter ש ['shin'], which, placed at the center of the Tetragrammaton, יהוה—the four letters of which represent the four branches of the cross—forms the pentagrammatic name יהשוה,[1] the significance of which we shall not stress here, as we only wish to point it out in passing. The five letters of the Pentagram are placed at the five points of the Blazing Star, a figure of the Quinary, which symbolizes more particularly the Microcosm, or individual man. The reason for this is as follows: if the Quaternary is taken to be Emanation, or the total manifestation of the Word, then each emanated being, a sub-multiple of this Emanation, will be characterized by the number four; it will be an individual being to the measure in which it is distinguished from Unity, or from the emanating center, and we have just seen that this distinction between the Quaternary and Unity is precisely the genesis of the Quinary.

In our study on the Demiurge we said that the distinction that gives birth to individual existence is the point of departure for Creation; indeed, the latter exists to the measure in which the totality of

1. *Yeshua*, the Hebrew form of 'Jesus'. Ed.

individual beings, characterized by the number five, is considered to be distinct from Unity, which gives birth to the number six. As we have seen earlier, this number can be considered as formed from two ternaries, the one the inverted reflection of the other; this is represented by the two triangles in the Seal of Solomon, symbol of the Macrocosm, or the created World.

Things are distinct from us to the degree that we distinguish between them; and it is precisely to this degree that they become external to us, as well as distinct from one another; from this point they appear clothed in forms, and this process of Formation, which is the immediate consequence of Creation, is characterized by the number that follows the Senary, namely the Septenary. We only need indicate the concordance of the preceding with the first chapter of Genesis: the six letters of the word בראשית, the six phases of Creation, and the formative role of the seven Elohim, representing the totality of natural forces, and symbolized by the seven planetary spheres, which latter could also be made to correspond to the first seven numbers, the lowest sphere, that of the Moon, being designated as the World of Formation.

The Septenary, such as we have just considered it, can be represented either by the double triangle and its center, or by a seven-pointed star, around which are inscribed the signs of the seven planets; this is the symbol of the forces of nature, that is, of the Septenary in the dynamic state. If it were considered in the static state, it could be seen as formed by the reunion of a Ternary and a Quaternary, and it would then be represented by a square surmounted by a triangle. Much could be said on the meaning of all these geometric forms, but such considerations would take us too far afield from the subject of our present study.

The process of Formation leads to what one can call material realization, which for us marks the limit of the manifestation of Being, which will then be characterized by the number eight. This number corresponds to the terrestrial World contained within the seven planetary spheres, and which be should be taken here as symbolizing the whole of the material World (each World is of course not to be understood as a place, but rather as a state or modality of being). The number eight also corresponds to an idea of equilibrium, because material realization is, as we have just said, a limitation, a halting point as it were with respect to the distinctions we create in things, the degree of these distinctions being a measure of what is symbolically designated as the depth of the fall. We have already said that the fall is nothing other than a means of expressing precisely this distinction that created individual existence, separating us from principial Unity.

In its static state, the number eight is represented by two squares, one inscribed within the other in such a way that the vertices of the inner square intersect the sides of the outer. In its dynamic state it is symbolized by two crosses with the same center, oriented in such a way that the branches of one bisect the right angles formed by the branches of the other.

If the number eight is added to Unity, it forms the number nine. For us this new number serves to limit the manifestation of Being, since it corresponds to material realization distinguished from Unity; it will therefore be represented by the circle, and will designate Multiplicity. We have said elsewhere that this circle, the points of which, indefinite in number, represent the formal manifestations of Being—we do not go further and say all manifestations, only the formal manifestations—can be regarded as Zero realized. Indeed, added to Unity the number nine forms the number ten, which also results from the union of Zero with the Unit, and which is represented by the circumference of the circle taken together with its center.

On the other hand, the Novenary could also be envisaged as a triple Ternary; from this, the static point of view, it will be represented by three superimposed triangles, each the reflection of the one immediately above, such that the intermediate triangle is inverted. This figure is the symbol of the three Worlds and their relationships; this is why the Novenary is often considered the number of hierarchy.

Finally, the Decad, corresponding to the circumference of the circle together with its center, is the total manifestation of Being, the complete development of Unity. It can therefore be regarded as nothing other than Unity realized within Multiplicity. Starting from it, the sequence of numbers begins again, forming a new cycle:

$$11 = 10 + 1;\ 12 = 10 + 2;\ \ldots\ 20 = 10 + 10$$

Then comes a third cycle, and so on indefinitely. Each of these cycles can be regarded as reproducing the first, but at another level, or, if one wishes, in another modality; they will therefore be symbolized by as many circles placed parallel one above another, in different planes; but since in reality there is no point of discontinuity between them, it is necessary that they be open circles, so that the end of each will at the same time be the beginning of the next. They will then not be circles, but the successive spirals of a helix traced on a cylinder, and these spirals will be indefinite in number, the cylinder itself being indefinite; and each spiral is projected as a circle onto a plane perpendicular to the axis of the cylinder, although in reality its point of departure and its point of arrival are not in the same plane. But we shall return to this subject in another study, when we come to the geometric representation of evolution.[2]

We must now consider another mode of production for numbers, production by multiplication, and more particularly the multiplication of a number by itself, giving birth successively to various powers of the number. But here the geometric representation would lead us to considerations concerning the dimensions of space, which it is preferable to study separately; we would then have to consider in particular the successive powers of the Decad, which would lead us to consider the question of the limits of the indefinite in a new light, as well as the question of passage from the indefinite to the Infinite.

In the preceding remarks, we have simply wished to indicate how the production of numbers starting from Unity symbolizes the different phases of the manifestation of Being in logical succession starting from the principle, Being itself, taken as identical to Unity; and if Zero—preceding primordial Unity—is introduced, one can thus even ascend beyond Being to Non-Being, that is, even to the Absolute.

2. See *The Symbolism of the Cross* and *The Multiple States of the Being*. Ed.

TRADITIONAL SCIENCES AND ARTS

1

INITIATION AND THE CRAFTS

WE HAVE OFTEN SAID that the 'profane' conception of the sciences and the arts, such as is now current in the West, is a very modern one and implies a degeneration with respect to a previous state where both presented an altogether different character. The same can also be said of the crafts; moreover, the distinction between arts and crafts, or between 'artist' and 'artisan', is also specifically modern, as if it were born of this profane deviation and had no meaning outside of it. For the ancients, the *artifex* is indifferently a man who practices either an art or a craft; but in truth he is neither artist nor craftsman in the current sense of these words, but something more than either, for, at least originally, his activity is related to principles of a far more profound order.

In every traditional civilization all activity of man, whatever it might be, is always considered as essentially deriving from principles; by this it is as if 'transformed', and instead of being reduced to what it is as a simple outer manifestation (which, in short, is the profane point of view) it is integrated in the tradition; and for the one who accomplishes it, it constitutes a means of participating effectively in this tradition. Even from a simple exoteric point of view this is the case: if, for example, one looks at a civilization like that of Islam or the Christian civilization of the Middle Ages, it is easy to see the 'religious' character which the most ordinary acts of existence assume. There religion is not something that holds a place apart, unconnected with everything else, as it is for modern Westerners (those at least who still consent to acknowledge a religion); on the contrary, it pervades the entire existence of the human being, or, better yet, all that constitutes this existence; and social life in particular is included in its domain, so much so that in such conditions there cannot really be anything 'profane', except for those who for one reason or another are outside of the tradition and whose case is then a simple anomaly. Elsewhere, when there is nothing to which the name of religion can properly be applied, there is nonetheless a traditional and 'sacred' legislation which, while having different characteristics, exactly fulfills the same role; these considerations can therefore be applied to all traditional civilizations without exception. But there is something more: if we pass from exoterism to esoterism (we use these words here for the sake of greater convenience, although they do not equally suit every case), we notice very generally the existence of an initiation bound up with and based on the crafts. These crafts are therefore still susceptible of a higher and more profound meaning; and we would like to point out how they can effectively furnish a way of approach to the initiatic domain.

What allows the above to be better understood is the notion of what the Hindu doctrine calls *svadharma*, that is to say the performance by each being of an activity in conformity with its own nature, and it is this notion, or rather its absence, that most clearly marks the shortcomings of the profane conception. According to the latter a man can adopt any profession, and he can even change it at will, as if this profession were something purely exterior to him, without any real connection with what he truly is, with what makes him himself and not another. In the traditional conception, on the contrary, everyone must normally fulfill the function for which he is destined by his very nature, and he cannot fulfill any other function without a resulting grave disorder, which will have its repercussion on the whole social organization to which he belongs. Even more than this, if such a disorder becomes general, it will have its effects on the cosmic realm itself, all things being linked together according to strict correspondences. Without dwelling further on this last point, which, however, could be quite easily applied to the conditions of the present time, we will note that the opposition of the two conceptions can, at least in a certain connection, be reduced to that of a 'qualitative' and a 'quantitative' point of view: in the traditional conception, it is the essential qualities of beings which determine their activities; in the profane conception, individuals are considered as interchangeable 'units', as if in themselves they were without any quality of their own. This last conception, which is obviously closely connected to modern ideas of 'equality' and 'uniformity' (the latter being literally against true unity, for it implies the pure and 'inorganic' multiplicity of a kind of social 'atomism'), can logically lead only to the exercise of a purely 'mechanical' activity, in which nothing specifically human subsists; this is in fact what we can see today. It must therefore be well understood that the 'mechanical' crafts of the moderns, being but a product of the profane deviation, can in no way offer the possibilities of which we intend to speak here; strictly speaking, they cannot even be considered crafts if one wishes to preserve the traditional meaning of this word, which is the only meaning with which we are concerned here.

If the craft is something of the man himself, and like a manifestation or expansion of his own nature, it is easy to understand that, as we were just saying, it can serve as a basis for an initiation, and even that in most cases it is what is best adapted to this end. Indeed, if initiation essentially aims at going beyond the possibilities of the human individual, it is equally true that it can only take this individual such as he is as its starting-point. This accounts for the diversity of initiatic ways, that is to say of the means implemented by way of 'supports', in conformity with the difference of individual natures, this difference subsequently arising ever less as the being advances on its way. The means thus employed can be efficacious only if they correspond to the very nature of the beings to whom they are applied. Because one must necessarily proceed from the more accessible to the less accessible, from the exterior to the interior, it is normal to take these means as the activity by which this nature is outwardly manifested. However, it goes without saying that this activity can play such a role only inasmuch as it really expresses the inner nature; it is thus truly a question of 'qualification' in the initiatic sense of this term. In normal conditions this 'qualification' should be a necessary condition for the very exercise of the craft. At the same time this touches on the fundamental difference which separates initiatic teaching from profane teaching: what is simply 'learned' from outside is here without any value.

What is in question is the 'awakening' of the latent possibilities that the being bears in itself (and this is basically the true significance of Platonic 'reminiscence').

These last considerations can further help us understand how initiation, taking the craft as its 'support', will at the same time, and inversely, as it were, have a repercussion on the exercise of this craft. The individual, having fully realized the possibilities of which his professional activity is but an external expression, and thus possessing the effective knowledge of what is the very principle of this activity, will henceforth consciously fulfill what had hitherto been only a quite 'instinctive' consequence of his nature. Thus, if for him initiatic knowledge is born of the craft, the latter, in its turn will become the field of application of this knowledge, from which it can no longer be separated. There will henceforth be a perfect correspondence between the interior and the exterior, and the work produced will no longer be only the expression to a certain degree and in a more or less superficial way, but a truly adequate expression of the one who will have conceived and executed it, and it will constitute a 'masterpiece' in the true sense of this word.

As can be seen, this is very far from the so-called unconscious or subconscious 'inspiration' in which moderns wish to see the criterion of the true artist, while considering him superior to the artisan, according to the more than contestable distinction that normally applies. Artist or artisan, anyone who acts under such an 'inspiration' is in any case only a profane person. No doubt, he shows by his 'inspiration' that he carries within himself certain possibilities, but as long as he has not effectively become aware of them, even if he attains to what is fittingly called 'genius', this changes nothing. Unable as he is to control these possibilities, his success will be so to speak accidental, which, moreover, is commonly recognized by saying that the 'inspiration' is sometimes lacking. All that can be conceded in order to reconcile the case under discussion to that in which true knowledge operates, is that the work which, consciously or unconsciously, truly flows from the nature of the one who performs it, will never give the impression of being a more or less painful effort which, because it is something abnormal, always leads to some imperfection. On the contrary, such a work will draw its very perfection from its conformity to nature, which implies directly and so to speak necessarily that it is exactly suited to the end for which it is destined.

If we now want a more rigorous definition of the sphere of what can be called the craft initiations, we will say that they belong to the 'lesser mysteries', referring to the development of the possibilities that belong properly to the human state, which is not the final aim of initiation, but at least constitutes the first obligatory phase. This development must first be accomplished in full, so as then to allow the surpassing of this human state; but beyond this, it is evident that individual differences which these craft initiations emphasize disappear completely and no longer play any role. As we have explained on other occasions, the 'lesser mysteries' lead to the restoration of what the traditional doctrines designate as the 'primordial state'. Once the being has reached this state, which still belongs to the sphere of human individuality, and which is the point of communication between it and the superior states, the differentiations which give rise to the various 'specialized' functions have disappeared, although all these 'specialized' functions also had their source there, or rather by this very means, and it is really a question of returning to this common source so as to possess in its plenitude all that is implied by the exercise of any function whatsoever.

If we view the history of humanity as taught by the traditional doctrines in conformity with the cyclical laws, we must say that since in the beginning man had full possession of his state of existence, he naturally had the possibilities corresponding to all the functions prior to every distinction of these latter. The division of these functions came about in a later phase, representing a state already inferior to the 'primordial state', but in which every human being, while having as yet only certain determined possibilities, still spontaneously had the effective consciousness of these possibilities. It was only in a period of the greatest obscuration that this consciousness became lost. From this point initiation became necessary to enable man to regain, along with this consciousness, the former state in which it inhered; this is the first of its aims, at which it aims most immediately. For this to be possible what is implied is a transmission going back by an unbroken 'chain' to the state to be restored, and thus, step by step, to the 'primordial state' itself; yet initiation does not stop there, for since the 'lesser mysteries' are only the preparation for the 'greater mysteries', that is to say for the taking possession of the superior states of the being, it is necessary to go back even beyond the origins of humanity. In fact, there is no true initiation, even to the most inferior and elementary degree, without the intervention of a 'non-human' element, which, as we have already explained in other articles, is the 'spiritual influence' regularly communicated by the initiatic rite. If this is so, there is obviously no place to search 'historically' for the origin of initiation, a search which now appears as bereft of meaning, nor, moreover, for the origin of the crafts, arts, and sciences viewed according to their traditional and 'legitimate' conception, since by means of multiple but secondary differentiations and adaptations they too all derive from the 'primordial state', which contains them all in principle. In this way they link up with other orders of existence beyond humanity itself, which moreover is necessary so that each according to its rank and measure can contribute effectively to the realization of the plan of the Great Architect of the Universe.

2

ON MATHEMATICAL NOTATION

WE HAVE OFTEN had occasion to remark that in reality most of the profane sciences—the only sciences the moderns know or even consider possible—represent only simple, distorted residues of the ancient, traditional sciences in the sense that the lowest part of these sciences, having ceased to have contact with the principles, and having thereby lost its true, original significance, ended up undergoing an independent development and came to be regarded as a branch of knowledge sufficient unto itself. In this respect, modern mathematics is no exception if one compares it to what was for the ancients the science of numbers and geometry; and when we speak here of the ancients, it is necessary to include therein even those of 'classical' antiquity, as the least study of Pythagorean and Platonic theories suffices to show, or at least should were it not necessary to take into account the extraordinary incomprehension of those who claim to interpret them today. Were this incomprehension not so complete, how for example could one maintain a belief in the 'empirical' origin of the sciences in question? For in reality— and to the contrary—they appear all the more removed from any 'empiricism' the further back one goes in time, and this is moreover equally the case for all other branches of scientific knowledge.

Modern mathematicians seem to have become ignorant of what number truly is, for they reduce their entire science to calculation, which for them means a mere collection of more or less artificial processes, and this amounts to saying, in short, that they replace number with the numeral; moreover, this confusion between the two is today so widespread that it can be found everywhere, even in everyday language. Now a numeral is strictly speaking no more than the clothing of a number; we do not even say its body, for it is rather the geometric form that in certain respects, can legitimately be considered to constitute the true body of a number, as the theories of the ancients on polygons and polyhedrons show when seen in the light of the symbolism of numbers. We do not mean to say, however, that numerals themselves are entirely arbitrary signs, the form of which has been determined only by the fancy of one or more individuals; there must be both numerical and alphabetical characters (the two not being distinguished in some languages moreover) and the notion of a hieroglyphic, that is, an ideographic or symbolic origin, can be applied to the one as well as to the other, and this holds for all scripts without exception.

What is certain is that mathematicians employ in their notation symbols the meaning of which they no longer understand, and which are like vestiges of forgotten traditions; and what is more serious, not only do they not ask themselves what this meaning might be, they even seem not to want them to have any at all. Indeed, they tend more and more to regard all notation as mere 'convention', by which they mean something set out in an entirely arbitrary manner, which in reality is a veritable impossibility, for one never establishes a convention without having some reason for doing so, and for doing precisely that rather than anything else. A convention can appear arbitrary only to those who are ignorant of this reason, and this is exactly what happens in this instance. Likewise, it is all too easy to pass from a legitimate and valid use of a notation to an illegitimate use that no longer corresponds to anything real, and that can even sometimes be completely illogical; this may seem strange when it is a question of a science like mathematics, which should have a particularly close relationship with logic, yet it is nevertheless all too true that one can find many illogicalities in mathematical notions as they are commonly understood.

One of the most striking examples of these illogical notions is that of the so-called mathematical infinite, which, as we have amply explained on other occasions, can in reality be no more than the indefinite—and let it not be believed that this confusion of the infinite and the indefinite can be reduced to a mere question of words.

What mathematicians represent by the sign ∞ can in no way be the Infinite understood in its true sense; the sign ∞ is itself a closed figure, therefore visibly finite, just like the circle, which some people have wished to make a symbol of eternity. In fact, the circle can only be a representation of a temporal cycle, indefinite merely in its order, that is to say, of what is properly called perpetuity; and it is easy to see that this confusion of eternity with perpetuity corresponds exactly to that of the infinite with the indefinite. In fact, the indefinite is only a development of the finite; but the Infinite cannot be derived from the finite. Furthermore, the Infinite is no more quantitative than it is determined, for quantity, being only a special mode of reality, is thereby essentially limited. What is more, the idea of an infinite number, that is to say a number greater than all other numbers according to the definition given by mathematicians, is an idea contradictory in itself, for however great a number n might be, the number $n+1$ will always be greater in virtue of the law of formation for the indefinite sequence of numbers. This contradiction leads to many others, as various philosophers have noted, although they never saw the full import of this argument, for they believed they could apply to the metaphysical Infinite what applies only to the false mathematical infinite, and thus they fell prey to the same confusion as their adversaries, only in an opposite direction. It is obviously absurd to wish to define the Infinite, for every definition is necessarily a limitation, as the words themselves show clearly enough, and the Infinite is that which has no limits; to seek to place it within a formula, or, in short, to clothe it in a form, is to attempt to place the universal All within one of its minutest parts, which is manifestly impossible. Finally, to conceive of the Infinite as a quantity is not only to limit it, as we have just said, but in addition it is to conceive of it as subject to increase and decrease, which is no less absurd. With similar considerations one quickly finds oneself envisaging several infinites that coexist without confounding or excluding one another, as well as infinites greater or smaller than other infinites; and, the infinite no longer sufficing, one even invents the 'transfinite', that is, the domain of quantities greater than the infinite: so many words and so many absurdities, even with regard to simple, elementary logic. Here we intentionally speak of 'invention', for if the realities of the mathematical order, like all other realities, can only be discovered and not invented, it is clear that this is no longer the case when, by a 'game' of notation, one allows oneself to be led into the domain of pure fantasy; but how could one hope for mathematicians to understand this difference when they willingly imagine that the whole of their science is and must be no more than a 'construction of the human mind', although if this were true it would of course reduce their science to a mere trifle?

What we said concerning the infinitely great, or what is so called, is equally true of what is no less improperly called the infinitely small: however small a number $1/n$ might be, the number $1/n+1$ will be smaller still; later we shall return to the question of what exactly this notation should be taken to mean. In reality, there is thus neither an infinitely great nor an infinitely small; but one can envisage the sequence of numbers as increasing and decreasing indefinitely in such a way that the so-called mathematical infinite will only be the indefinite, which, let us say again, proceeds from the finite, and is consequently always reducible to it. The indefinite is thus still finite, which is to say limited; even if we do not know its limits, or are incapable of determining them, we do know that they exist, for every indefinitude pertains only to a certain order of things, limited precisely by the existence of other things outside of it. By the same token, one can obviously envisage a multitude of indefinites; one can even add them to each other, or multiply them by each other, which naturally leads to the consideration of indefinites of unequal magnitude, and even different orders of indefinitude, in both the increasing direction and the decreasing direction. Once this is understood, we shall be able to see the real significance of the previously mentioned absurdities, which disappear as soon as the so-called mathematical infinite is replaced with the indefinite; but whatever might be obtained thus will of course have no relation to the Infinite, and will always be rigorously null with respect to it; and the same may be said of all ordinary finitude, of which the indefinite is necessarily but an extension. At the same time, these considerations also show in a precise way the impossibility of arriving at synthesis by analysis: however much one adds together an indefinite number of elements successively, one will never obtain the All, because the All is infinite, and not indefinite; it cannot be conceived of as other than infinite, for it could only be limited by something outside of itself, and then it would not be the All. If it can be said that it is the sum of all its elements, this is only on the condition that the word 'sum' be taken in the sense of an integral, which is not calculated by taking its elements one by one; and even were one to suppose that one or more indefinite sequences could be passed through analytically, one would not for that have advanced a single step from the point of view of universality, and one would always be at exactly the same point in relation to the Infinite. Moreover, all of this can be applied analogically to other domains than quantity; and the immediate consequence is that profane science, of which the points of view and methods are exclusively analytical, is by that very fact incapable of transcending certain limitations; here the imperfection is not simply inherent in its present state, as some have wished to believe, but in its very nature, that is, ultimately, in its lack of principles.

We have said that the sequence of numbers can be considered indefinite in two directions, the increasing and the decreasing; but this demands some further explanation, for an objection can immediately be raised. True number, what one might call pure number, is essentially whole number; and the sequence of whole numbers, starting from the unit, continues ever to increase, but it progresses entirely in a single direction, and thus the other, opposite direction—that of indefinite decrease—cannot be represented by it. However, one is brought to consider various other kinds of number aside from the whole numbers; these, it is usually said, are extensions of the idea of number, and this is true after a certain fashion; but at the same time these extensions are also distortions, which is what mathematicians seem too easily to forget on account of their 'conventionalism', which causes them to misunderstand the origin and raison d'être of these numbers. In fact, numbers other than whole numbers always appear first and foremost as the representation of the results of operations that would be impossible were one to keep to the point of view of pure arithmetic, which, in all strictness, is the arithmetic of whole numbers alone. Indeed, one does not arbitrarily consider the results of the aforementioned operations thus, instead of regarding them purely and simply as impossible; generally speaking, it is in consequence of the application made of number—discontinuous quantity—to the measurement of magnitudes belonging to the order of continuous quantity. Between these modes of quantity there is a difference of nature such that a correspondence between the two cannot be perfectly established; to remedy this to a certain degree, at least insofar as it is possible, one seeks to reduce, as it were, the intervals of this discontinuity constituted by the sequence of whole numbers, by introducing between its terms other numbers, such as fractional and incommensurable numbers, which would be meaningless apart from this consideration. Moreover, it must be said that in spite of this something of the essentially discontinuous nature of number will inevitably always remain, preventing one from thus obtaining a perfect equivalent to the continuous. The intervals can be reduced as much as one might like—that is, in short, they can be reduced indefinitely—but they cannot be eliminated; thus one is once again brought to consider a certain aspect of the indefinite, and this could find its application in a study of the principles of the infinitesimal calculus, although this is not what we propose to do at present.

Under these conditions and with these reservations, one can accept certain of these extensions of the idea of number to which we have just alluded, and give them, or rather restore to them, a legitimate significance; thus, notably, we can consider the inverses of the whole numbers represented by symbols of the form $1/n$ and forming the indefinitely decreasing sequence, symmetrical to the indefinitely increasing sequence of whole numbers. We must further note that although the symbol $1/n$ could evoke the idea of fractional numbers, the numbers in question here are not defined as such; it suffices for us to consider the two sequences as constituted by numbers respectively greater and smaller than the unit, that is, by two orders of magnitude having their common limit in the unit, while at the same time both can be regarded as having issued from this unit, which is indeed the primary source of all numbers. Since we have spoken of fractional numbers, we should add in this connection that the definition ordinarily given to them is again absurd: in no way can fractions be 'parts of a unit', as is said, for the true unit is necessarily indivisible and without parts; arithmetically, a fractional number represents no more than the quotient of an impossible division; but this absurdity arises from a confusion of the arithmetical unit with what are called 'units of measurement', which are units only by convention, since in reality they are magnitudes of another sort than number. The unit of length, for example, is only a certain length chosen for reasons foreign to arithmetic, to which one makes the number 1 correspond in order to be able to measure all other lengths by reference to it; but by its very nature as continuous magnitude, all length, even when thus represented numerically by unity, is no less always and indefinitely divisible. Comparing it to other lengths, one might therefore have to consider parts of this unit of measurement, without it in any way being necessary that they be parts of the arithmetical unit; and it is only thus that the consideration of fractional numbers is really introduced, as a representation of the ratios of magnitudes that are not exactly divisible by one another. The measurement of a magnitude is in fact no more than the numerical expression of its ratio to another magnitude of the same species taken as the unit of measurement, or, basically, as the term of comparison; and from this one sees that all measurement is essentially founded on division, something which could give rise to further observations which are important, but beyond our present subject.

That said, we can now return to the double numerical indefinitude constituted in the increasing direction by the sequence of whole numbers, and in the decreasing direction by that of their inverses; both sequences start from the unit, which alone is its own inverse, since $1/1 = 1$. Moreover, there are as many numbers in one sequence as there are in the other, such that if one considers the two indefinite sets as forming a unique sequence, one could say that the unit occupies the exact mid-point within this sequence of numbers; indeed, for every number n in one sequence, there will correspond another number $1/n$ in the other, such that $n \times 1/n = 1$, any two inverse numbers multiplied together again producing the unit. To generalize further, if we wished to introduce fractional numbers instead of considering only the sequence of whole numbers and their inverses as we have just done, nothing would be changed in this regard: on one side there would be all the numbers greater than the unit, and on the other all those smaller than the unit; here, again, for any number $a/b > 1$, there will be a corresponding number $b/a < 1$ in the other set, and reciprocally, such that $a/b \times b/a = 1$, and there will thus be exactly the same number of terms in each of these two indefinite groups separated by the unit. One can say further that the unit, occupying the mid-point, corresponds to the state of perfect equilibrium, and that it contains in itself all numbers, which proceed from it in pairs of inverse or complementary numbers, each pair, by virtue of its complementarity, constituting a relative unity in its indivisible duality. In what follows we shall further examine the consequences implied by these various considerations.

If one considers the sequence of whole numbers together with that of their inverses, in accordance with what was said above, the first will be indefinitely increasing and the second indefinitely decreasing; one could say that the numbers thus tend on the one side toward the indefinitely great and on the other toward the indefinitely small, understanding by this the very limits of the domain in which one considers these numbers, for a variable quantity cannot but tend toward a limit. The domain in question is, in short, that of numerical quantity taken in every possible extension; this amounts to saying that its limits are not determined by such and such a particular number, however great or small one might suppose it to be, but solely by the nature of number as such. By the same token number, like everything else of a determined nature, excludes all that it is not, and thus there can be no question of any infinite here; moreover, we have just said that the indefinitely great must inevitably be conceived of as a limit, and in this connection one can point out that the expression 'tend toward infinity', employed by mathematicians in the sense of 'increase indefinitely', is again an absurdity, since the infinite obviously implies the absence of all limits, and since consequently there is nothing toward which it is possible to tend. It goes without saying that the same observations can be applied to modes of quantity other than number, that is, to different kinds of continuous quantity, notably the spatial and the temporal; each of these is likewise capable of indefinite extension within its order, but essentially limited by its very nature, as, moreover, is quantity itself in all its generality; the very fact that there exist things to which quantity is not applicable suffices to demonstrate the contradiction in the idea of the so-called 'quantitative infinite'.

Furthermore, when a domain is indefinite, we cannot know its limits distinctly, and, consequently, we will not be able to fix them in a precise manner; here, in short, we have the entire difference between indefinitude and ordinary finitude. There thus remains a sort of indeterminacy, but one which is such only from our point of view and not in reality itself, since its limits are no less existent on that account; whether we see them or not in no way changes the nature of things. As far as number is concerned, one could also say that this apparent indeterminacy results from the fact that the sequence of numbers in its entirety is not 'terminated' by a certain number, as is always the case with any given portion of the sequence considered in isolation; there is thus no number, however great it might be, that can be identified with the indefinitely great in the sense in which we take it; and parallel considerations naturally apply to the indefinitely small. However, one can at least regard a number as practically indefinite, if one may so express it, when it can no longer be expressed by language or represented in writing, which indeed occurs the moment one considers numbers that go on ever increasing or decreasing; here we have simply a matter of 'perspective', if one wishes, but even this is in accordance with the character of the indefinite, which is ultimately nothing other than that of which the limits can be, not done away with—which would be impossible, since the finite can only produce the finite—but simply pushed back to the point of being entirely lost from view.

In this regard certain rather curious questions arise: thus, one could ask why the Chinese language symbolically represents the indefinite by the number ten thousand; the expression 'the ten thousand beings', for example, means all beings, which in reality are an indefinite multitude. What is most remarkable is that precisely the same thing occurs in Greek, where a single word likewise serves to express both ideas at once, with a simple difference in accentuation, which is obviously only a quite secondary detail: μύριοι, 'ten thousand'; μυρίοι, 'an indefinitude'.[1] The true reason

1. The English cognate *myriad* has come to combine both meanings. Ed.

for this is as follows: the number ten thousand is the fourth power of ten; now according to the formulation of the *Tao Te Ching*, 'one produced two, two produced three, three produced all numbers,' which implies that four, produced immediately after three, is in a way equivalent to the whole set of numbers, and this because, when one has the quaternary, by adding the first four numbers one also has the decad, which represents a complete numerical cycle: $1+2+3+4=10$; this is the Pythagorean Tetraktys, the significance of which we shall perhaps return to more thoroughly on another occasion. One can further add that this representation of numerical indefinitude has its correspondence in the spatial order: raising a number from one power to the next highest power represents in this order, the addition of a dimension; now, since our space has only three dimensions, its limits are transcended when one goes beyond the third power. In other words, this amounts to saying that elevation to the fourth power marks the very term of its indefinitude, since, as soon as it is effected, one has thereby departed from this extension.

Be that as it may, it is in reality the indefinitely great that mathematicians represent by the sign ∞, as we have said; if the sign did not have this meaning, it would have none at all; and according to the preceding, what is thus represented is not a determined number, but as it were an entire domain, which, moreover, is necessary for it to be possible to envisage inequalities and even different orders of magnitude within the indefinite, as we have already pointed out.

As for the indefinitely small, which can similarly be regarded as embracing everything in the decreasing order that is found to lie outside the limits of our means of evaluation, and which as quantity we are consequently led to consider practically non-existent with respect to us, one can represent it in its own set by the symbol 0—although this is in fact only one of the meanings of zero—without bringing in here the notation of differential or infinitesimal quantity, which essentially finds its justification only in the study of continuous variations; and it must be understood that this symbol no longer represents a determined number for the same reasons as those given for the indefinitely great.

The sequence of numbers such as we have been considering it, extending indefinitely in the two opposite directions of increase and decrease and composed of the whole numbers and their inverses, presents itself in the following form: $0 \ldots 1/4, 1/3, 1/2, 1, 2, 3, 4 \ldots \infty$; two numbers equidistant from the central unit will be inverses or complementaries of one another, thus producing the unit when multiplied together, as we explained earlier: $1/n \times n = 1$, such that, for the two extremities of the sequence, one would be compelled to write $0 \times \infty = 1$ as well. However, since the signs 0 and ∞, the two factors of this product, do not really represent determined numbers, it follows that the expression $0 \times \infty$ itself constitutes what is called an indeterminate form, and must then be written: $0 \times \infty = n$, where n could be any number; but in any case one is thus brought back to ordinary finitude, the two opposed indefinites being so to speak neutralized by one another. Here, once again, one can clearly see that the symbol ∞ most emphatically does not represent the Infinite, for the Infinite can have neither opposite nor complement, and it cannot enter into correlation with anything whatsoever, no more with zero than with the unit or with any number; as the absolute All, it contains Non-Being as well as Being, such that zero itself, whenever it is not regarded as purely nothing, must necessarily be considered to be contained within the Infinite.

In alluding here to Non-Being, we touch on another meaning of zero, quite different from the one we have just been considering, and moreover one that is more important from the point of view of metaphysical symbolism; but in this regard, in order to avoid all confusion between the symbol and that which it represents, it is necessary to make it quite clear that the metaphysical Zero, which is Non-Being, is no more the zero of quantity than metaphysical Unity—which is Being—is the arithmetical unit; what is designated by these terms is so only by analogical transposition, since as soon as one places oneself within the Universal, one is obviously outside of all special domains such as that of quantity. Moreover, it is not insofar as it represents the indefinitely small that zero can be taken as a symbol of Non-Being, but rather insofar as, following another of its mathematical meanings, it represents the absence of quantity, which in its order indeed symbolizes the possibility of non-manifestation, just as the unit symbolizes the possibility of manifestation, since it is the point of departure for the indefinite multiplicity of number, as Being is the principle of all manifestation.

In whatever manner zero is envisaged, it can in no case be taken to be purely nothing, which is all too obvious when it is a question of the indefinitely small; it is true that this is only a derivative sense so to speak, owing to a sort of approximate assimilation of quantities that are negligible for us to the total absence of quantity; but insofar as it is a question of this absence of quantity itself, which is null in this connection, it is quite clear that it cannot be so in all respects, as is apparent in an example like that of the point, which is without extension, that is, spatially null, but which is as we have explained elsewhere nonetheless the very principle of all extension. It is truly strange, moreover, that mathematicians are for the most part inclined to envisage zero as purely nothing, when at the same time it is impossible for them not to regard it as endowed with an indefinite potentiality, since, placed to the right of another, 'significant' digit, it helps to form the representation of a number that, precisely by the repetition of this zero, can increase indefinitely, as for example with the number ten and its successive powers; if zero really were absolutely nothing, this could not be so, and it would even be a useless sign, entirely deprived of real value; here we have yet another inconsistency to add to the list of those we have already pointed out so far.

Returning now to zero considered as a representation of the indefinitely small, what is important is to keep in mind the fact that within the doubly indefinite sequence of numbers, the domain of the latter embraces all that eludes our means of evaluation in a certain direction, just as within the same sequence the domain of the indefinitely great embraces all that eludes our means of evaluation in the other direction. This being said, to speak of numbers less than zero is obviously no more appropriate than to speak of numbers greater than the indefinite; and it is still more unacceptable—if such is even possible—when zero simply represents the absence of quantity, for it is totally inconceivable that a quantity should be less than nothing; this, however, is what is attempted—although in a slightly different sense than the one just discussed—when the consideration of so-called negative numbers is introduced into mathematics, forgetting that these numbers were originally no more than an indication of the result of a subtraction impossible in reality, in which a greater number is taken away from a smaller; but this subject of negative numbers, and the logically contestable consequences it entails, calls for further discussion.

Ultimately, the consideration of negative numbers arises solely from the fact that when a subtraction is arithmetically impossible, its result is nonetheless not devoid of meaning when linked to magnitudes that can be reckoned in two opposite directions, as, for example, distances or times. From this results the geometric representation habitually accorded negative numbers: on a straight line, the distances lying along it are considered to be positive or negative depending on whether they fall in one direction or the other, and a point is chosen to serve as the origin, in relation to which the distances are positive on one side and negative on the other, the origin itself being given a coefficient of zero; the coefficient of each point on the line will thus be the number representing its distance from the origin, and its sign of + or – will simply indicate on which side the point falls on in relation to the origin; with a circle one could likewise designate positive and negative directions of rotation, which would give rise to analogous remarks. Furthermore, as the line is indefinite in both directions, one is lead to consider both a positive and a negative indefinite, represented by the signs $+\infty$, and $-\infty$ respectively, commonly designated by the absurd expressions 'greater infinity' and 'lesser infinity'. One might well ask what a negative infinity would be, or again what could remain were one to take away an infinite amount from something, or even from nothing, since mathematicians regard zero as nothing. In cases such as these one has only to put the matter in clear language in order to immediately see how devoid of meaning they are. We must further add that, particularly when studying the variation of functions, one might next be led to believe that the negative and the positive indefinite merge, such that a moving object, departing from its origin and moving further and further away in the positive direction would return toward the origin from the negative side if the movement were carried on for an indefinite amount of time, or vice versa, whence it would result that the straight line, or what is so considered, would in reality be a closed line, albeit an indefinite one. One could show, moreover, that the properties of the straight line in a plane would be entirely analogous to those of a diameter on the surface of a sphere, and that the plane and the straight line could thus be likened respectively to a sphere and a circle of indefinitely great radius, ordinary circles in the plane then being comparable to the smaller circles on the sphere; without pushing the issue further, we shall only note that here one can grasp the precise limits of spatial indefinitude directly, as it were; if one wishes to maintain some semblance of logic, how then can one still speak of the infinite in all of this?

When considering positive and negative numbers as we have just done, the sequence of numbers takes the following form: $-\infty \ldots -4, -3, -2, -1, 0, 1, 2, 3, 4 \ldots +\infty$, the order of these numbers being the same as that of the corresponding points on the line, that is, the points having these numbers for their respective coefficients. Although the sequence is just as indefinite in either direction, it is completely different from the one we envisaged earlier: it is symmetric not with respect to 1, but to 0, which corresponds to the origin of the distances; and two numbers equidistant from the central term again reproduce it, but this time by 'algebraic' addition—that is, by addition performed while taking account of signs, which in this case would amount, arithmetically speaking, to a subtraction—and not by multiplication. One can immediately see a disadvantage that inevitably results from the artificial—we do not say arbitrary—character of this notation: if one takes the unit as the point of departure, the entire sequence of numbers will immediately follow from it; but, if one takes zero, it is on the contrary impossible to derive any number from it, the reason for this being that in reality the forming of the sequence would then be based on considerations of a geometric rather than an arithmetical order, and also that, in consequence of the difference in nature of the quantities treated in these two branches of mathematics, there can never be a completely rigorous correspondence between arithmetic and geometry, as we have already said. Moreover, the new sequence in no way increases indefinitely in one direction and decreases indefinitely in the other, as was the case with the preceding series; or at least, if one claims to consider it thus, it is only in a most incorrect 'manner of speaking'. In reality, the sequence increases indefinitely in both directions equally since it is the same sequence of whole numbers that is contained on either side of the central zero; what is called the 'absolute value'—another rather singular expression, as the quantities in question are always of an essentially relative order—must be taken into consideration only in a purely quantitative respect, the positive or negative signs changing nothing in this regard, since they express no more than differences in 'situation', as we have just now explained. The negative indefinite is thus by no means comparable to the indefinitely small; on the contrary, just like the positive indefinite, it belongs with the indefinitely great; the only difference is that it proceeds in another direction, which is perfectly conceivable when it is a question of spatial or temporal magnitudes, but totally devoid of meaning in the case of arithmetical magnitudes, which proceed solely in one direction since they are nothing other than the magnitudes of which the sequence of numbers is composed. Negative numbers are by no means numbers 'less than zero', which essentially is but a pure and simple impossibility, and the sign by which they are designated can in no way reverse the order in which they are ranked with respect to their magnitude. Moreover, in order to realize it as clearly as possible, it suffices to note that the point of the coefficient –2, for example, is further from the origin than the point of the coefficient –1, and not less far, as would inevitably be the case were the number –2 in fact less than the number –1; in reality, it is not the distances themselves, insofar as they are capable of being measured, that can be qualified as negative, but only the direction in which they lie; here we have two entirely different things, and it is precisely the confusion of the two that is the source of a large part of the logical difficulties raised by the notation of negative numbers.

Among the other bizarre and illogical consequences of this notation, let us draw attention to the question of so-called 'imaginary' quantities, introduced in the solving of algebraic equations; these quantities are presented as the roots of negative numbers, which again could answer only to an impossibility; perhaps some other meaning could be assigned to them, whereby they might correspond to something real, but in any case, their theory and application to analytic geometry as presented by contemporary mathematicians hardly appears as anything but a veritable mass of confusions and even absurdities, and as the outcome of a need for excessive and artificial generalizations, a need that does not draw back even at manifestly contradictory propositions; certain theorems concerning the 'asymptotes of a circle', for example, amply suffice to prove that this remark is by no means an exaggeration. One could say, it is true, that this is no longer a question of geometry strictly speaking, but only of algebra translated into geometric terms; but precisely because such translation, as well as its inverse, is possible to a certain degree, it is extended to cases in which it can no longer mean anything, for this is indeed the symptom of an extraordinary confusion of ideas, as well as the extreme result of a 'conventionalism' that goes so far as to cause a loss of the sense of all reality.

There is yet more to be said, and before ending we shall now turn to the consequences, also quite contestable, of the use of negative numbers from the point of view of mechanics; indeed, since in virtue of its object the field of mechanics is in reality a physical science, the very fact that it is treated as an integral part of mathematics has not failed to introduce certain distortions. In this regard we shall only say that the so-called 'principles' upon which modern mathematicians build this science such as they conceive of it (and among the various abuses of the word 'principles', this is not the least worthy of remark) are in fact only more or less well-grounded hypotheses, or again, in the most favorable case, only more or less simple, general laws, perhaps more general than others, but still no more than applications of true universal principles in a highly specialized domain. Without entering into excessively long explanations, let us cite, as an example of the first case, the so-called 'principle of inertia', which nothing justifies, neither experience, which on the contrary shows that inertia has no role in nature, nor the understanding, which cannot conceive of this so-called inertia consisting only in a complete absence of properties; rigorously speaking, such a word could only be applied to pure potentiality, but this latter is assuredly something altogether different from the quantified and qualified 'matter' envisaged by physicists. An example of the second instance may be seen in what is called the 'principle of the equality of action and reaction', which is so little a principle as to follow immediately from the general law of the equilibrium of natural forces: whenever this equilibrium is in any way disturbed, it immediately tends to re-establish itself, whence a reaction of which the intensity is equivalent to that of the action that provoked it; it is therefore only a simple, particular case of 'concordant actions and reactions', a principle that does not concern the corporeal world alone, but indeed the totality of manifestation in all its modes and states; and it is precisely on this question of equilibrium that we propose to dwell for a little while.

Two forces in equilibrium are usually represented by two opposed 'vectors', that is, by two line segments of equal length, but of opposite directions; if two forces applied to the same point have the same intensity and fall along the same line, but in opposite directions, they are in equilibrium. As they are then without action at their point of application, it is even said that they cancel each other out, although this ignores the fact that if one of the forces is suppressed, the other will immediately act, proving that they were never really annulled in the first place. The forces are characterized by numerical coefficients proportional to their respective intensities, and two forces of opposite direction are given coefficients with different signs, the one positive, the other negative: the one being f, the other $-f'$. In the case just considered, in which the two forces are of the same intensity, the coefficients characterizing them must be equal with respect to their 'absolute values'; one then has: $f=f'$, from which can be derived the condition for their equilibrium: $f-f'=0$, which is to say that the sum of the two forces, or of the two 'vectors' representing them, is null, such that equilibrium is thus defined by zero. Now zero having been incorrectly regarded by mathematicians as a sort of symbol for nothing—as if nothing could be symbolized by something—it seems to follow that equilibrium is the state of non-existence, which is a rather strange conclusion; nonetheless, it is almost certainly for this reason that instead of saying that two forces in equilibrium neutralize one another, which would be more exact, it is said that they annul one another, which is contrary to the reality of things, as we have just made clear by a most simple observation.

The true notion of equilibrium is entirely different. In order to understand it, it suffices to point out that all natural forces—and not only mechanical forces, which, let us say again, are no more than a very particular case—are either attractive or repulsive; the first can be considered compressive forces, or forces of contraction, and the second expansive forces, or forces of dilation. Given an initially homogenous medium, it is easy to see that for every point of compression there will necessarily correspond an equivalent expansion at another point, and conversely, such that two centers of force, neither of which could exist without the other, will always have to be considered correlatively. This is what can be called the law of polarity, and it is applicable to all natural phenomena, since it is derived from the duality of the very principles that preside over all of manifestation; in the domain with which physicists occupy themselves, this law is evident above all in electrical and magnetic phenomena. Now if two forces, the one compressive, the other expansive, act upon the same point, then the condition requisite for them to be in equilibrium or to neutralize one another, that is, the condition which, when fulfilled, will produce neither contraction nor dilation, is that the intensities of the two forces be equivalent—we do not say equal, since they are of different species. The forces can be characterized by coefficients proportional to the contraction or dilation they produce, in such a way that if one considers a compressive force and an expansive force together, the first will have a coefficient $n > 1$, the second a coefficient $n' < 1$; each of these coefficients will be the ratio of the density of the space surrounding the point in consideration under the action of the corresponding force, to the original density of the same space, which is taken to be homogenous when not subject to any forces, in virtue of a simple application of the principle of sufficient reason. When neither compression nor dilation is produced, the ratio will inevitably equal one, since the density of the space will be unchanged; in order for two forces acting upon a point to be in equilibrium, their resultant must have a coefficient of one. It is easy to see that the coefficient of this resultant is the product—and not the sum, as in the 'classical' conception—of the coefficients of the two forces under consideration; these two coefficients, n and n', must therefore each be the inverse of the other: $n' = 1/n$, and we will then have as the condition for equilibrium, $(n)(n') = 1$; thus equilibrium will no longer be defined by zero, but by the unit.

It will be seen that the definition of equilibrium with respect to the unit—which is the only real definition—corresponds to the fact that the unit occupies the mid-point in the doubly indefinite sequence of whole numbers and their inverses, while this central position is as it were usurped by zero in the artificial sequence of positive and negative numbers. Far from being the state of non-existence, equilibrium is on the contrary existence considered in and of itself, independent of its secondary, multiple manifestations; moreover, it is certainly not Non-Being, in the metaphysical sense of the word, for existence, even in this primordial and undifferentiated state, is still the point of departure for all differentiated manifestations, just as the unit is the point of departure for the multiplicity of numbers. As we have just considered it, this unit, in which equilibrium resides, is what the Far-Eastern tradition calls the 'Invariable Middle'; and according to the same tradition, this equilibrium or harmony is the reflection of the 'Activity of Heaven' at the center of each state and of each modality of being.

We conclude this study, which makes no claim to be exhaustive, with a 'practical' conclusion; we have shown explicitly why the conceptions of modern mathematicians cannot inspire us with any more respect than do those of the representatives of the other profane sciences; their opinions and views thus have no weight in our eyes, and we need take no account of them in our evaluations of one or another theory, evaluations which, in this domain as well as any other, can be based for us only on the data of traditional knowledge.

3

THE ARTS AND THEIR TRADITIONAL CONCEPTION

WE HAVE FREQUENTLY emphasized the fact that the profane sciences are only the product of a relatively recent degeneration brought about by a misunderstanding of the ancient traditional sciences—or rather only of some of them—the others having completely fallen into oblivion. This is true not only for the sciences, but also for the arts, and furthermore the distinction between them was once far less accentuated than it is now; the Latin word *artes* was sometimes also applied to the sciences, and in the Middle Ages, the classification of the 'liberal arts' included subjects which the modern world would assign to either one or the other group. This one remark is already enough to show that art was once something other than what is now understood by this name, and that it implied a real knowledge with which it was incorporated, as it were, and this knowledge obviously could only have been of the order of the traditional sciences.

By this alone can one understand that in certain initiatory organizations of the Middle Ages, such as the 'Fedeli d'Amore', the seven 'liberal arts' were considered to correspond to the 'heavens', that is, to states which were identified with the different degrees of initiation.[1] For this the arts as well as the sciences had to be susceptible of a transposition giving them a real esoteric value; and what makes such a transposition possible is the very nature of traditional

1. See *The Esoterism of Dante*, chap. 2.

knowledge, which, whatever its order, is always connected to transcendent principles. This knowledge is thus given a meaning which can be termed symbolic, since it is founded on the correspondence that exists between the various orders of reality; but here it must be stressed that this does not involve something superadded to them accidentally, but on the contrary something that constitutes the profound essence of all normal and legitimate knowledge, and which, as such, is inherent in the sciences and the arts from their very beginning and remains so as long as they have not undergone any deviation.

That the arts can be viewed from this point of view should cause no astonishment, once one sees that the crafts themselves, in their traditional conception, serve as a basis for an initiation, as we have explained.[2] In this connection we should also recall that we spoke at that time about how the distinction between the arts and the crafts seems specifically modern and, in short, appears to be only a consequence of the same degeneration which has given birth to the profane outlook, for this latter literally expresses nothing other than the very negation of the traditional spirit. After all, whether it was a question of art or craft, there was always to one degree or another the application and the implementation of various sciences of a higher order, gradually linked to initiatic knowledge itself. Furthermore, the direct implementation of initiatic knowledge also went by the name of art, as can be seen clearly by expressions such as 'sacerdotal art' and 'royal art', which refer to the respective applications of the 'greater mysteries' and the 'lesser mysteries'.

Let us now consider the arts and give to this word a more limited and at the same time more customary meaning, that is, what is more precisely called the 'fine arts'. From the preceding we can say that each of them must constitute a kind of symbolic language adapted to the expression of certain truths by means of forms which are of the visual order for some, and of the auditive or sonorous order for others, whence their customary division into two groups, the 'plastic arts' and the 'phonetic arts'. In previous studies we have explained that this distinction, like that between two kinds of corresponding

2. See pt. 2, chap. 1 above, 'Initiation and the Crafts'.

rites founded on the same categories of symbolic forms, originally refers to the difference that exists between the traditions of a sedentary people and those of a nomadic people.[3] Moreover, whether the arts are of one or another genre, it is easy to see in a general way that in a civilization they have a character all the more manifestly symbolic as the civilization itself is more strictly traditional, for their true value then lies less in what they are in themselves than in the possibilities of expression which they afford, beyond those to which ordinary language is confined. In a word, their productions are above all destined to serve as 'supports' for meditation, and as foundations for as deep and extensive an understanding as possible, which is the very raison d'être of all symbolism;[4] and everything, even to the smallest details, must be determined by this consideration and subordinated to this end, without any useless addition emptied of meaning and simply meant to play a 'decorative' or 'ornamental' role.[5]

One sees that such a conception is as far removed as possible from all modern and profane theories, as for example that of 'art for art's sake', which fundamentally amounts to saying that art is what it should be only when it has no meaning, or again that of 'moralizing' art, which from the standpoint of knowledge is obviously of no greater value. Traditional art is certainly not a 'game', to use an expression dear to certain psychologists, nor is it simply a means of procuring for man a special kind of pleasure, qualified as 'superior', although no one really knows why, for as soon as it is only a question of pleasure, everything is reduced to purely individual preferences, among which no hierarchy can logically be established. Moreover, neither is it a vain and sentimental declamation, for which ordinary language is certainly more than sufficient without

3. See 'Cain and Abel' in *The Reign of Quantity and The Signs of the Times*, chap. 21, and also 'Rite and Symbol' in *Perspectives on Initiation*, chap. 16.

4. This is the Hindu notion of *pratīka*, which is no more an 'idol' than it is a work of imagination and individual fantasy. Each of these two Western interpretations, opposed to a certain extent, is as wrong as the other.

5. The degeneration of certain symbols into ornamental 'motifs' because the meaning has ceased to be understood is one of the characteristic features of the profane deviation.

there in any way being a need to resort to more or less mysterious or enigmatic forms, and in any case forms far more complicated than what they would have had to express. This gives us an opportunity to recall in passing—for one can never insist too much on these things—the perfect uselessness of 'moral' interpretations which certain people aim to give to all symbolism, including initiatic symbolism properly speaking. If it really were a question of such banalities, one does not see why or how one would ever have thought of 'veiling' them in some way, for they do very well without this when expressed by profane philosophy, and it would then be better to say quite simply that in reality there is neither symbolism nor initiation.

That said, one may ask on which of the various traditional sciences the arts most directly depend. This, of course, does not exclude their also having more or less constant relations with the others, for here everything necessarily holds together and is connected in the fundamental unity of the doctrine, which could neither be destroyed in any way, nor even affected by the multiplicity of its applications. The conception of sciences which are narrowly 'specialized' and entirely separated from each other is clearly antitraditional insofar as it manifests a lack of principle, and is characteristic of the 'analytic' outlook that inspires and rules the profane sciences, whereas any traditional point of view can only be essentially 'synthetic'. With this reservation, it can be said that what lies at the very heart of all the arts is chiefly an application of the science of rhythm under its different forms, a science which is itself immediately connected with that of number. It must be clearly understood that when we speak of the science of number, it is not a question of profane arithmetic as understood by the moderns, but of that arithmetic to be found in the Kabbalah and in Pythagorism (the best known examples), whose equivalent also exists, under varied expressions and with greater or lesser developments, in all the traditional doctrines.

What we have just said may appear especially obvious for the phonetic arts, the productions of which are all constituted by sequences of rhythms unfolding in time. Poetry owes its rhythmical character to having originally been the ritual mode of expression of the 'language of the gods', that is to say the 'sacred language' par excellence,[6] a function of which it still preserved something until a relatively recent time when 'literature' had still not been invented.[7] As for music, it will surely not be necessary to insist on this, since its numerical basis is still recognized by moderns themselves, distorted though it is through the loss of traditional data; formerly, as can be seen especially well in the Far East, modifications could only be introduced into music in consequence of certain changes occurring in the actual state of the world in accordance with cyclical periods, for musical rhythms were at once intimately linked with the human and social order and with the cosmic order, and in a certain way they even expressed the connections between the one and the other. The Pythagorean conception of the 'harmony of the spheres' belongs to exactly the same order of considerations.

For the plastic arts, the productions of which are developed through extension in space, the same thing cannot appear as immediately apparent, and yet it is no less strictly true; but rhythm is then as it were fixed in simultaneity, and not in a state of successive unfolding as in the previous case. This can be understood especially by observing that in this second group the typical and fundamental art is architecture, and in the final analysis the other arts, such as sculpture and painting—at least in regard to their original intention—are only simple dependencies thereof. Now, in architecture, rhythm is directly expressed by the proportions existing between the various parts of the whole, and also through geometric forms, which, when all is said and done are from our point of view only the spatial translation of numbers and their relations.[8] Here

6. See 'The Language of the Birds' in *Symbols of Sacred Science*, chap. 7.

7. It is rather curious to note that modern 'scholars' have come to an indiscriminate application of the word 'literature' to everything—even to the sacred scriptures, which they have the pretension to study in the same way as the rest and by the same methods—and, when they speak of 'biblical poems' or of 'Vedic poems', while completely misunderstanding what poetry meant for the ancients, their intention is again to reduce everything to something purely human.

8. In this connection, it should be noted here that Plato's 'geometer God' is properly identified with Apollo, who presides over all the arts; this, directly derived as it is from Pythagorism, has a particular importance concerning the filiation of certain traditional Hellenic doctrines and their connection with a 'Hyperborean' primal origin.

again, of course, geometry must be considered in a very different way from that of the profane mathematicians, and its anteriority in respect to the latter most completely refutes those who would like to attribute an 'empirical' and utilitarian origin to this science. On the other hand, we have here an example of the way in which, from the traditional point of view, the sciences are linked together to such an extent that at times they could even be considered the expressions, as it were, of the same truths in different languages. Furthermore, this is only a most natural consequence of the 'law of correspondences' which is the very foundation of all symbolism.

These few notions, summary and incomplete as they are, will at least suffice for an understanding of what is most essential in the traditional conception of the arts and what differentiates this conception most profoundly from a profane one with regard to the basis of these arts as applications of certain sciences, with regard to their significance as different modalities of symbolic language, and with regard to their intended role as a means for helping man to approach true knowledge.

4

THE CONDITIONS OF CORPOREAL EXISTENCE

According to the *Sāṇkhya* of Kapila, there are five *tanmātras* or elementary essences, ideally perceptible (or rather 'conceptible'), but incomprehensible and imperceptible under any mode of universal manifestation, because themselves unmanifested; for just this reason it is impossible to attribute to them particular designations, for they cannot be defined by any formal representation.[1] These *tanmātras* are potential principles, or, to use an expression recalling the doctrine of Plato, the 'ideas-archetypes' of the five elements of the physical material world, and thus, of course, of an indefinitude of other modalities of manifested existence corresponding analogically to these elements in the multiple degrees of this existence. According to the same correspondence, these principial ideas also potentially imply, respectively, the five conditions the combinations of which constitute the determinations of this particular possibility of manifestation that we call corporeal existence. Thus, the five *tanmātras* or principial ideas are the 'essential' elements, primordial causes of the five 'substantial' elements of physical manifestation, which are only particular determinations of exterior modifications. Under this physical modality, they are expressed in the five conditions according to which the laws of

1. They can only be designated by analogy with the different orders of sensible qualities, for it is only in this way that we can know them (indirectly, in some of their particular effects) as long as we belong, as individual and relative beings, to the world of manifestation.

corporeal existence are formulated;[2] the law, intermediate between the principle and the consequence, expresses the relation of cause and effect (relation in which the cause can be regarded as active and the effect as passive), or of the essence to the substance, considered as the א and the ת, the two extreme points of the modality of manifestation that are envisaged (and which, in the universality of their extension, are the same for each modality). But in themselves neither essence nor substance belong to the domain of this manifestation, any more than the two extremities of *yin-yang* are contained in the plane of the cyclic curve; they are on either side of this plane, and this is why, in reality, the curve of existence is never closed.

The five elements of the physical world[3] are, as we know, ether (*akāsha*), air (*vāyu*), fire (*tejas*), water (*apa*), and earth (*prithvī*); the order in which they are enumerated is that of their development, in accordance with the teaching of the *Veda*.[4] The effort has often been made to assimilate the elements to the different states or degrees of condensation of physical matter, starting with primordial homogenous ether, which fills the whole expanse, thus uniting between them all the parts of the corporeal world; from this point of view, proceeding from the densest to the most subtle, that is, in the inverse order of their differentiation, the earth is made to correspond to the solid state, water to the liquid state, air to the gaseous state, and fire to a still more rarefied state rather similar to the 'radiant state' recently discovered by the physicists and currently under investigation with the help of their special methods of observation and experimentation. This point of view undoubtedly contains a

2. However, the five *tanmātras* cannot be considered as being manifested by these conditions, any more than they can by the elements and the perceptible qualities that correspond to them; on the contrary, it is by the five *tanmātras* (considered as principle, support, and end) that all these things are manifested, followed by everything resulting from their unlimited combinations.

3. Each of these primitive elements is called *bhūta*, from *bhū* 'to be', more particularly in the sense of 'subsisting'; this term *bhūta* therefore implies a substantial determination, which in fact corresponds well to the notion of the corporeal element.

4. The origin of ether and air, not mentioned in the text of the *Veda*, where the genesis of the three other elements is described (*Chhāndogya Upanishad*), is indicated in another passage (*Taittirīya Upanishad*).

portion of truth, but it is too systematic, that is, too strictly particularized, and the order it establishes in the elements differs from the preceding on one point, for it places fire before air and immediately after ether, as if it were the first element to differentiate itself within the original cosmic milieu. On the contrary, according to the teaching that conforms to orthodox doctrine, air is the first element, and air, a neutral element (only potentially containing the active-passive duality), differentiating itself through polarization (bringing about this duality from potency to act), produces in itself fire, an active element, and water, a passive element (one could also say 'reactive', that is, acting in reflective mode, correlatively to action in spontaneous mode of the complementary element). The reciprocal action and reaction of fire and water gives birth (through a sort of crystallization or residual precipitation) to earth, the 'terminating and final element' of corporeal manifestation. More justifiably, we could consider the elements as different vibratory modalities of physical matter, modalities under which it makes itself perceptible successively (in purely logical succession, naturally)[5] to each of the senses of our corporeal individuality; moreover, all of this will be sufficiently explained and justified through the considerations we will bring out later in this study.

Above all, we must establish that ether and air are distinct elements, contrary to what is maintained by some heterodox schools;[6] but to make what we are going to say on this point more comprehensible, let us first recall that the five conditions taken together, to which corporeal existence is subject are space, time, matter, form, and life. Consequently, in order to set forth these five conditions in a single definition, it can be said that a body is 'a material form living in time and space'; let us add that when we use the expression

5. We cannot in any way consider such a concept as that of the ideal figure imagined by Condillac in his *Traité des Sensations*.

6. Notably the *Jainas*, the *Bauddhas* and the *Chārvākas*, with whom most of the Greek atomist philosophers are in accord on this point; an exception must be made however for Empedocles, who admitted the five elements but imagined them developing in the following order: ether, fire, earth, water, and air. We will not insist on this, however, for we do not intend to examine here the opinions of the different Greek schools of 'physical philosophy'.

'physical world', it is always as a synonym of 'domain of corporeal manifestation'.[7] It is only provisionally that we have enumerated these conditions in the preceding order, without prejudgment of relations between them, until in the course of our exposition we determine their respective correspondences with the five senses and the five elements, which, moreover, are all likewise subject to this set of five conditions.

[1] *Akāsha*, ether, considered as the most subtle element and the one from which all the others proceed (forming, in relation to its primordial unity, a quaternary of manifestation), occupies all physical space, as we have said;[8] however, it is not immediately through the ether that this space is perceived, its particular quality not being extension, but sound; this requires some explanation. In fact, ether, envisaged in itself, is originally homogenous; its differentiation, which engenders the other elements (beginning with air), takes its start from an elementary movement, originating at any point whatsoever, in this indeterminate cosmic milieu. This elementary movement is the prototype of the vibratory movement of physical matter. From the spatial point of view, it is propagated around its starting-point in isotropic mode, that is to say through concentric waves, in a helicoidal vortex along all the directions of space, forming the unclosed figure of an indeterminate sphere. To mark the connections which already link together the different conditions of corporeal existence as enumerated above, we will add that this spherical form is the prototype of all forms; it contains them all potentially, and its first differentiation in polarized mode can be represented by the figuration of *yin-yang*, which is easy to see if one refers back to the symbolic conception of Plato's Androgyne.[9]

7. The lack of adequate expressions in Western languages is often a great difficulty for the exposition of metaphysical ideas, as we have already noted on various occasions.

8. 'Ether, which is spread everywhere, enters simultaneously both the exterior and interior of things' (citation of Shankarāchārya, in 'The Demiurge', pt. 1, chap. 1 above.

9. This could even be supported by various embryological considerations, but to say more on this now would lead us too far from our present subject.

Movement, even when elementary, necessarily presupposes space, just as it does time, and one can even say that in a way it is the result of these two conditions, since it necessarily depends on them as the effect depends on the cause (in which it is implied potentially);[10] but it is not the elementary movement itself that gives us the direct perception of space (or more exactly of extension). In fact, it is important to note clearly that when we speak of movement produced in the ether at the origin of all differentiation, it is exclusively a question of elementary movement, a movement that we can call undulatory, or simple vibratory movement (the wave-length and the infinitesimal period) in order to indicate its mode of propagation, which is uniform in space and time, or rather the geometric representation of the latter. Only in considering the other elements will we be able to envisage complex modifications of this vibratory movement, modifications which correspond for us to various orders of sensations. This last point is all the more important in that on it lies the entire fundamental distinction between the characteristic qualities of ether and those of air.

We must now ask which among the corporeal sensations presents the perceptible exemplar of vibratory movement, which we perceive directly without its passing through one or another of the various modifications to which it is subject. Now, elementary physics itself teaches us that these conditions are fulfilled by sonorous vibrations, of which the wavelength, just as the speed of propagation,[11] falls within the limits of our sensory perception; one can thus say that it is the sense of hearing which directly perceives vibratory movement. It will doubtless be objected at this juncture that it is not the etheric vibration that is thus perceived in sonorous mode, but rather the

10. However, it is clear that in the spatial and temporal conditions which make its production possible, movement can only commence under the action (exteriorized activity, in reflective mode) of a principial cause, which is independent of these conditions (see further on).

11. Velocity in any movement is the relation at any given moment between the space traversed and the time elapsed in traversing it; and, in its general formulation, this relation (constant or variable according to whether the movement is uniform or not) expresses the law governing the movement under consideration (see below).

vibration of a gaseous, liquid, or solid medium. It is no less true that it is ether that forms the original medium of propagation of vibratory movement, which, in order to enter within the limits of perceptibility corresponding to the range of our auditive faculty, must be amplified only by its propagation through a denser medium (ponderable matter), without for all that losing its characteristic of simple vibratory movement (in this case, however, its wavelength and frequency are no longer infinitesimal). In order thus to manifest the sonorous quality, it is necessary that this movement already possess it potentially (directly)[12] in its original medium, ether, of which consequently this quality, in its potential state (of primordial indifferentiation), really constitutes its characteristic nature in relation to our corporeal sensibility.[13]

On the other hand, if one investigates by which of the five senses time is more particularly manifested to us, it is easy to see that it is the sense of hearing; moreover, this is a fact that can be verified experimentally by all those who are accustomed to examining the respective origins of their various perceptions. The reason is as follows: for time to be perceived materially (that is, for it be in contact with matter, particularly as regards our corporeal organism), it must be measurable, for in the physical world this is a general characteristic of all perceptible quality (when considered as such).[14]

12. It also potentially possesses the other sensory qualities as well, but indirectly, since it can manifest them—that is, produce them in act—only through different complex modifications (amplification being on the contrary only a simple modification, the first of all).

13. Moreover, this same sonorous quality belongs equally to the other four elements, no longer as their own or characteristic quality, but insofar as they all proceed from ether. Each element, proceeding immediately from the one preceding it in the order of their successive development, is perceptible to the same senses as the latter, and, in addition, to another sense which corresponds to its own particular nature.

14. This characteristic is implied by the presence of matter among the conditions of physical existence; but, in order to realize measure, it is to space that we must link all the other conditions, as we have here for time. We measure matter itself by division, and it is divisible only insofar as it is extended, that is to say situated in space (see further on for the demonstration of the absurdity of the atomist theory).

Now, for us it is not direct because it is not in itself divisible, and we only conceive the measure through division, at least in the usual and perceptible way (for one can conceive of other modes of measure, such as integration for example). Time will therefore be rendered measurable only insofar as it expresses itself according to a divisible variable, and as we shall see further on, this variable can only be space, divisibility being a quality essentially inherent to the latter. Consequently, in order to measure time it will be necessary to envisage it insofar as it enters into contact with space, as it is combined therewith, as it were, and the result of this combination is the movement by which space is traversed, which, being the sum of a series of elementary displacements envisaged in successive mode (that is, precisely under the temporal condition), is a function[15] of the time elapsed to traverse it. The relation existing between this space and this time expresses the law of movement under consideration.[16] Conversely, time will then likewise be expressed in relation to space, by reversing the previously considered relation between these two conditions in a determined movement; this amounts to considering this movement as a spatial representation of time. The most natural representation will be that which represents it numerically by the simplest function; it will therefore be a uniform oscillatory movement (rectilinear or circular), one, that is, with a constant velocity or oscillatory period, which can be regarded as no more than a sort of amplification (implying moreover a differentiation in relation to the directions of space) of the elementary vibratory movement. But since this is also the characteristic of sonorous vibration, we see immediately by this that it is hearing which, among the senses, particularly gives us the perception of time.

We must now observe that even if space and time are the necessary conditions of movement, they are not its first causes; they are themselves the effects by means of which is manifested movement, itself another effect (secondary in relation to the preceding ones,

15. In the mathematical sense of a quantity that varies according to the value of another quantity.

16. This is the formula of velocity, of which we have spoken earlier, and which, considered for each moment (that is to say, for the infinitesimal variations of time and space), represents the derivative of space in relation to time.

which can be regarded in this sense as its immediate causes since it is conditioned by them) of the same essential causes, causes which potentially contain the integrality of all their effects, and are synthesized in the total and supreme Cause conceived as the unlimited and unconditioned Universal Power.[17] On the other hand, for movement to actually occur, there must be something which is moved, in other words a substance (in the etymological sense of the word)[18] on which it is exercised; that which is moved is matter, which thus

17. This is clearly expressed in biblical symbolism: as regards the special cosmogonic application to the physical world, *Cain* ('the strong and powerful transformer, the one who centralizes, seizes and assimilates to himself') corresponds to time, *Abel* ('the gentle and peaceful liberator, the one who withdraws and calms, who vanishes, who flees the center'), to space, and *Seth* ('the base and the basis of things') to movement (see the works of Fabre d'Olivet [esp. *Cain* (New York: G.P. Putnam's Sons, 1923)], Ed). The birth of *Cain* precedes that of *Abel*, which is to say that the perceptible manifestation of time precedes (logically) that of space, just as sound is the perceptible quality which develops first; the murder of *Abel* by *Cain* represents then the apparent destruction—in the exteriority of things—of simultaneity by succession. The birth of *Seth* is consecutive to this murder, as conditioned by what it represents, but *Seth*, or movement, does not proceed in itself from *Cain* and *Abel*, or from time and space, although its manifestation is a consequence of the action of one on the other (hence regarding space as passive in relation to time); but, like them, he is born from *Adam* himself, that is, that he proceeds as directly as do they from the exteriorization of the powers of Universal Man, who has, as Fabre d'Olivet says, 'generated, in the midst of its integrating faculty, its reflective shadow.'

Time, under its three aspects of past, present, and future, unites between them all the modifications—considered as successive—of each of the beings that it leads through the Current of Forms toward the final Transformation; thus *Shiva*, under the aspect of *Mahādeva*, having three eyes and holding the *trishūla* (trident), keeps to the center of the Wheel of Things. Space, product of the expansion of the potentialities of a principial and central point, makes the multiplicity of things coexist in its unity; now these things, considered (exteriorly and analytically) as simultaneous, are all contained in it and penetrated by ether, which entirely fills space. Likewise, *Vishnu* under the aspect of *Vāsudeva*, manifests things, penetrating them in their intimate essence through multiple modifications distributed along the circumference of the Wheel of Things, without the Unity of its supreme Essence being altered (cf. *Bhagavad Gītā*, 10). Finally, movement, or better, 'mutation', is the law of all modification or diversification in the manifested order, a cyclic and evolutive law, which manifests *Prajāpati* or *Brahmā* considered as 'Lord of the Creatures' at the same time that it is 'the Provider of Substance [*Substanteur*] and organic Sustainer'.

18. But not in the sense understood by Spinoza.

does not intervene in the production of movement except as a purely passive condition. The reactions of matter are subject to movement (since passivity always implies a reaction) and develop in matter the different perceptible qualities, which, as we have already said, correspond to the elements the combinations of which constitute this modality of matter (considered as object, not of perception, but of pure conception)[19] that we know as the 'substratum' of physical manifestation. In this domain, activity is therefore neither inherent nor spontaneous in matter, but belongs to it in a reflexive fashion insofar as this matter coexists with space and time; and it is this activity of matter in movement which constitutes, not life in itself, but the manifestation of life in the domain that we are considering. The first effect of this activity is to give form to this matter, for it is necessarily formless so long as it is in a homogenous and undifferentiated state, which is that of primordial ether; it is only capable of taking on all the forms potentially contained within the integral extension of its particular possibility.[20] It can thus be said that it is also movement that determines the manifestation of form in physical or corporeal mode; and, just as all form proceeds from the spherical primordial form by differentiation, so all movement can be reduced to a set of elements each of which is a vibratory helicoidal movement differing from the elementary spherical vortex only in that space will no longer be envisaged as isotropic.

We have already had occasion to consider the five conditions of corporeal existence taken as a whole, and we will have to return to this subject from different points of view as we consider each of the four elements the respective characteristics of which remain to be studied.

[2] *Vāyu* is air, and more particularly air in movement (or considered as principle of differentiated movement[21] since in its original meaning this word really means breath or wind); mobility is thus

19. Cf. the dogma of the 'Immaculate Conception' (see 'Pages dedicated to Sahaïf Ataridiyah', by Abdūl-Hādi, in *La Gnose*, January 1911, p35).

20. See 'The Demiurge', pt. 1, chap. 1 (citation from the *Veda*).

21. As we shall see, this differentiation implies above all the idea of one or several specialized directions in space.

considered as the characteristic nature of this element,[22] which is the first to be differentiated from the primordial ether (and which, like ether, is still neutral, the exterior polarization appearing by duality as the complementarity Fire and Water, and not before). In fact, this first differentiation necessitates a complex movement, constituted by a series (combination or coordination) of elementary vibratory movements, and determining a rupture of the homogeneity of the cosmic milieu by propagating itself according to certain particular and determined directions from its point of origin. Once this differentiation takes place, space must no longer be regarded as isotropic; on the contrary, it can then be related to a complex of several defined directions taken as axes of coordinates, and which, serving to measure it in any portion of its extension—and even, theoretically, in the totality of the latter—are what one calls the dimensions of space. These coordinate axes (at least according to the ordinary idea of so-called 'Euclidean' space, which corresponds directly to the sensible perception of corporeal extension) will be three orthogonal diameters of the indeterminate spheroid that comprise the full extension of its deployment, and their center can be any point of this extension, which latter will then be considered as the product of the development of all spatial virtualities contained in this point (principially indeterminate). It is important to note that the point in itself is not contained in space and cannot in any way be conditioned by it, because on the contrary it is the point that creates out of its own 'ipseity' redoubled or polarized into essence and substance,[23] which amounts to saying that it contains space

22. The word *Vāyu* derives from the verbal root *vā*, 'to go', 'to move' (which is still retained in the French *il va*, whereas the roots *i* and *gā*, which are linked to the same idea, are found respectively in the Latin *ire* and the English *to go*). Analogically, the atmospheric air, considered as milieu surrounding our body and affecting our organism, is rendered perceptible to us by its displacement (kinetic and heterogeneous state) before we perceive its pressure (static and homogenous state). Let us recall that *Aer* (from the root אר, which is more especially related to rectilinear movement) signifies 'that which gives to everything the principle of movement,' according to Fabre d'Olivet.

23. In the field of manifestation considered, essence is represented as the center (initial point), and substance as the circumference (indefinite surface of terminal expansion from this point); cf. the hieroglyphic meaning of the Hebraic particle את, formed of the two extreme letters of the alphabet.

potentially. It is space that proceeds from the point, and not the point that is determined by space; but secondarily (all manifestation or exterior modification being only contingent and accidental in relation to its 'intimate nature'), the point determines itself in space in order to realize the actual extension of its potentialities of unlimited multiplication (of itself by itself). Again, one can say that this primordial and principial point fills all of space by the deployment of its possibilities (envisaged in active mode in the point itself dynamically 'effecting' the extension, and in passive mode in this same extension realized statically). It is situated in space only when it is considered in each particular position that it is able to occupy, that is to say in each of its modifications corresponding precisely to each of its special possibilities. Thus extension already exists in the potential state in the point itself; it starts to exist in the actual state only when this point, in its first manifestation, is in a way doubled in order to stand face to face with itself, for one can then speak of the elementary distance between two points (although in principle and in essence the latter are only one and the same point), whereas, when one considers only a single point (or rather when one considers the point only under the aspect of principial unity), it could obviously not be a question of distance. However, one must point out that the elementary distance is only what corresponds to this doubling in the domain of spatial or geometric representation (which only has the character of symbol for us). Metaphysically, the point is considered to represent Being in its unity and its principial identity, that is to say *Ātmā* outside of any special condition (or determination) and all differentiation; this point itself, its exteriorization (which can be considered as its image, in which it is reflected) and the distance that joins them while at the same time separating them, and that marks the relationship existing between both (a relationship that implies causality, indicated geometrically by the direction of the distance, envisaged as a 'directed' segment, and going from point-cause to point-effect), corresponds respectively to the three terms of the ternary that we have distinguished in Being considered as knowing itself (that is to say in *Buddhi*), terms which, outside this point of view, are perfectly identical among themselves, and which are designated *Sat, Chit*, and *Ānanda.*

We say that the point is the symbol of Being in its Unity; this latter can in fact be conceived in the following way: if the extension of a dimension, or a line, is measured quantitatively by a number a, the quantitative measure of the extension in two dimensions, or of the surface, will be of the form a^2, and that of the extension in three dimensions, or of volume, will be of the form a^3. Thus, adding a dimension to the extension is equivalent to raising by one the exponent of the corresponding quantity (which is the measure of this extension), and, inversely, to take away a dimension from the extension is equivalent to diminishing this very exponent by one. If the last dimension, that of the line (and, consequently, the final unity of the exponent), is removed, it remains the point geometrically, and numerically it remains a^0, that is, from the algebraic point of view, unity itself, which identifies quantitatively the point of this unity. It is therefore an error to believe, as some do, that the point can only correspond numerically to zero, for it is already an affirmation, that of Being pure and simple (in all its universality). No doubt it has no dimension, because in itself it is not situated in space, which latter contains, as we have said, only the indefinitude of its manifestations (or of its particular determinations); since it is without dimension, it obviously no longer has any form; but to say that it is non-formal is by no means to say that it is nothing (zero is considered thus by those who assimilate the point to it), and moreover, although without form, it contains space potentially, which, realized in actuality, will in its turn be the container of all forms, at least in the physical world.[24]

24. In a wholly elementary way one can even take account of the development of spatial potentialities contained in the point by observing that the displacement of the point engenders the line, as likewise that of the line engenders the surface, and the surface in turn engenders volume. However, this point of view presupposes the realization of extension, and even of extension in three dimensions, for clearly each of the elements considered successively can only produce the following one by moving in a dimension that is actually exterior to it, and in relation to which it was already situated. On the contrary, all these elements are realized simultaneously—time then no longer intervening—in and through the original deployment of the indefinite and unclosed spheroid we have considered, a deployment that is effected not in actual space, whatever this may be, but in a pure void deprived of all positive attribution, and which is in no way productive by itself, but which, in passive

We have said that extension exists in actuality once the point has manifested itself by its self-exteriorization, since it is by this very act that the point realizes space. It should not be thought that this assigns a temporal beginning to space, however, for it is a question of a purely logical starting-point only, of an ideal principle of space understood in the fullness of its extension, and not limited to corporeal extension alone.[25] Time intervenes only when the two positions of the point are envisaged as successive, while on the other hand the relation of causality that exists between them implies their simultaneity; and it is also insofar as this first differentiation is envisaged under the aspect of succession, that is, in temporal mode, that the resulting distance (as intermediary between the principial

---

potential, is full of all that the point contains in active potential (being thus, in a way, the negative aspect of *that* of which the point is the positive aspect). This void, thus filled in an originally homogenous and isotropic way with the virtualities of the principial point, will be the milieu—or, if you will, the 'geometric place'—of all the modifications and ulterior differentiations of the latter, thus being in relation to universal manifestation what ether is particularly for our physical world. Envisaged in this way, and in this plenitude that it holds integrally from the expansion (in exteriorizing mode) of the point's active potentialities (which are themselves all the elements of this plenitude), it *is*. Without this plenitude it would not be, since the void can only be conceived as 'non-entity', and thus it is entirely differentiated from the 'universal void' (*sarva shūnya*) of the Buddhists, who, moreover, attempting to identify it with ether, regard the latter as 'non-substantial' and consequently do not count it as one of the corporeal elements. Moreover, the true 'universal void' would not be this void just considered, which is capable of containing all the possibilities of Being (symbolized spatially by the virtualities of the point), but is, quite to the contrary, everything outside of Being, where there can no longer in any way be a question of 'essence' or of 'substance'. This would then be Non-Being or metaphysical zero, or, more exactly, an aspect of Non-Being, which, moreover, is full of everything that in total Possibility is not subject to any development in exterior or manifested mode, and which is thereby absolutely inexpressible.

25. Corporeal extension is the only one known to astronomers, and even then they can only study a certain portion of it by their methods of observation. Moreover, this is what produces for them the illusion of the so-called 'infinity of space', for by the effect of a veritable intellectual myopia that seems inherent to all analytical science, they are induced to consider as 'to infinity' [*sic*] everything that exceeds the range of their sensory experience, and which in relation to them and the domain that they study, is in reality no more than simple indefinity.

point and its exterior reflection, the first by implication being immediately situated in relation to the second)[26] can be regarded as measuring the amplitude of elementary vibratory movement, of which we have spoken previously.

However, without the coexistence of simultaneity with succession, movement itself would not be possible, for then the mobile point (or at least considered as such in the course of its process of modification) would be there where it is not, which is absurd, or it would not be anywhere, which amounts to saying that there would not actually be any space where movement can in fact occur.[27] Ultimately all the arguments that have been raised against the possibility of movement, notably by certain Greek philosophers, amount to this, and it is this question, moreover, that most embarrasses academicians and modern philosophers. Its solution is very simple, however, and as we have already indicated elsewhere, lies precisely in the coexistence of succession and simultaneity, succession in the modalities of manifestation, in the actual state, but simultaneity in principle, in the potential state, making possible the logical linking of causes and effects (every effect being implied and contained potentially in its cause, which is in no way affected or modified by the actualization of this effect).[28] From the physical point of view, the idea of succession is tied to the temporal condition and the idea of simultaneity to the spatial condition;[29] movement, in its passage

26. This localization already implies, moreover, a first reflection preceding the one that we shall consider here but with which the principial point identifies itself (by determining itself) in order to make of it the effective center of extension in the process of realization, and from which it is then reflected in all the other points (purely virtual in relation to it) of this extension, which is its field of manifestation.

27. The point is in fact 'somewhere' once it is situated or determined in space (its potentiality in passive mode)—so as to realize this space, that is—and in this very realization, which all movement, even elementary movement, necessarily presupposes, to bring it from potency to act.

28. Leibnitz seems to have caught at least a glimpse of this solution when he formulated his theory of 'pre-established harmony', which has generally been very poorly understood by those who have tried to interpret it.

29. Leibnitz respectively defines time and space by means of these two notions, which are wholly ideal when envisaged outside of this specialized point of view, under which alone they are rendered perceptible.

from potency to act, results from the union or the combination of these two conditions, and reconciles (or balances) the two corresponding ideas, by making a body coexist with itself in simultaneous mode from the purely spatial point of view (which is essentially static), identity thus being conserved through all its modifications, contrary to the Buddhist theory of 'total dissolubility'. This coexistence underlies an indefinite series of positions (which are so many modifications of this same body, and are accidental and contingent in relation to what constitutes its intimate reality, in substance as in essence), positions which are successive from the temporal point of view (kinetic in its relation with the spatial point of view).[30]

On the other hand, since actual movement supposes time and its coexistence with space, we are led to the following formulation: a body can move according to one or another of the three dimensions of physical space, or following a direction that is a combination of these three dimensions, for whatever the direction (fixed or variable) of its movement, it can always be reduced to a more or less complex series of components related to the three axes of the coordinates to which is linked the space under consideration; but in every case this body moves always and necessarily in time. As a result, time will become another dimension of space if one changes succession into simultaneity; in other words, to suppress the temporal condition amounts to adding a supplementary dimension to physical space, of which the new space thus obtained constitutes a prolongation or extension. This fourth dimension thus corresponds to 'omnipresence' in the domain considered, and it is through this transposition in 'non-time' that we can conceive the 'permanent actuality' of the manifested Universe. While noting that

30. It is quite evident, in fact, that all these positions coexist simultaneously insofar as they are places situated in one and the same extension, of which they are only different portions (quantitatively equivalent, moreover), all equally capable of being occupied by one and the same body, which on the one hand must be envisaged statically in each of these positions when considered in isolation in relation to the others, and also, on the other hand, when all of them are considered as a whole outside the temporal point of view.

all modification is not assimilable to movement, which is only an exterior modification of a special order, this also explains all the phenomena commonly regarded as miraculous or supernatural[31]—quite mistakenly, since they still belong to the domain of our present individuality in one or the other of its multiple modalities, for the corporeal individuality constitutes only a very small part thereof, a domain in which the conception of 'fixed time' allows us to embrace fully all indefinitude.[32]

31. There are facts that seem inexplicable only because in searching for an explanation one does not move outside the ordinary conditions of physical time. Hence it is said that the sudden reconstitution of injured organic tissues that is observed in certain cases regarded as 'miraculous' cannot be natural because it is contrary to the physiological laws of the regeneration of these tissues, which laws operate through multiple and *successive* generations (or bipartitions) of cells, and necessarily require the collaboration of time. First, it is not proved that a regeneration of this kind, as sudden as it may be, is truly *instantaneous*, that is, not actually requiring *any time* in order to occur, and it is possible that in certain circumstances the multiplication of the cells is simply rendered much more rapid than in normal cases, to the point of no longer requiring even the least duration detectable to our sensory perception. Next, even in admitting that it is really a question of a truly *instantaneous* phenomenon, there is still the possibility that in certain particular conditions differing from the ordinary, but nonetheless quite natural, this phenomenon is in fact accomplished *outside of time* (implying the 'instantaneity' in question, which, in the cases considered, amounts to the *simultaneity* of the multiple cellular bipartitions, or at least as expressed in its corporeal or physiological correspondence), or, if one prefers, that it is accomplished *in 'non-time'*, whereas in ordinary conditions it is accomplished *in time*. It would no longer be a miracle for the person who could understand its real meaning and resolve the following question, which is much more paradoxical in appearance than it is in reality: how, while living *in the present*, can we act so that any event produced *in the past* has not happened? And it is essential to note that this (which is not more impossible *a priori* than it is to *presently* prevent the realization of an event *in the future*, since the link of succession is not a causal link) does not in any way suppose a return to the past as such (such a return being a manifest impossibility since it would equally be a transport into the future as such), since there is obviously neither past nor future in relation to the 'eternal present'.

32. In this connection, we might add a remark on the numeric representation of this indefinitude (continuing to take it under its spatial symbol): the line is measured, that is to say represented quantitatively by a number a to the first power; but since its measure may also be taken using decimal division as basis, one can write $a = 10n$. In this case, then, one will have for the surface: $a^2 = 100n^2$, and for the volume: $a^3 = 1000n^3$; for the extension to four dimensions, it will again be necessary to

Let us return to our conception of the point filling all of space through the indefinitude of its manifestations, that is to say of its multiple and contingent modifications. From the dynamic point of view[33] the latter must be considered in space (of which they are all the points) as so many centers of force (of which each is potentially the very center of space), and force is nothing other than the affirmation in manifested mode of the will of Being, symbolized by the point. In the universal sense, this will is the active power or 'productive energy' (*Shakti*)[34] of Being indissolubly united to itself, and exerted on the actional domain of Being, that is to say, using the same symbolism, on space itself envisaged passively, that is, from the static point of view (as the field of action of any one of these centers of force).[35] Thus, in all its manifestations and in each of

---

add a factor a, giving: $a^4 = 10{,}000n^4$. Furthermore, it can be said that all the powers of 10 are contained virtually in its fourth power, just as the denary, complete manifestation of unity, is contained in the quaternary

33. It is important to point out that 'dynamic' is in no way synonymous with 'kinetic'; the movement may be considered as the consequence of a certain action of force (thus rendering this action measurable by means of a spatial translation permitting a definition of its 'intensity'), but it cannot be identified with this force itself. Furthermore, under other modalities and in other conditions, the force (or the will) in action obviously produces something completely different from movement, since, as we have just pointed out above, the latter constitutes only a particular case among the indefinitude of possible modifications comprised in the exterior world, that is, in the whole of universal manifestation.

34. Moreover, this active power can be envisaged under different aspects: as creative power, it is more particularly called *Kriyā-Shakti*, whereas *Jñāna-Shakti* is the power of knowledge, *Ichchhā-Shakti* the power of desire, and so on, considering the unlimited multiplicity of attributes manifested by Being in the exterior world, but for all that without in any way dividing the unity of Universal Potency in itself—which is necessarily correlative with the essential unity of Being, and is implied by this very unity—into the plurality of these aspects. — In the psychological order, this active power is represented by אשה, 'volitional facility' of איש, the 'intellectual man' (see Fabre d'Olivet, *The Hebraic Tongue Restored*).

35. Universal Possibility, regarded in its integral unity (but, of course, as to the possibilities of manifestation only), as the feminine side of Being (of which the masculine side is *Purusha*, which is Being itself in its supreme and 'non-acting' identity in itself), is thus polarized here into active potency (*Shakti*) and passive potency (*Prakriti*).

them, the point can be regarded in relation to these manifestations as being polarized in active and passive mode, or, if one prefers, direct and reflected mode;[36] the dynamic, active, or direct point of view corresponds to essence, and the static, passive, or reflective point of view corresponds to substance;[37] but of course the consideration of these two complementary points of view in every modality of the manifestation in no way alters the unity of the principial point (any more than of Being, of which it is the symbol), and this allows one clearly to conceive the fundamental identity of the essence and the substance, which, as we said at the beginning of this study, are the two poles of universal manifestation.

Extension, considered from the substantial point of view, is not distinct as regards our physical world from the primordial ether (*akāsha*), so long as it does not produce therein a complex movement determining a formal differentiation; but the indefinitude of possible combinations of movements then gives birth in this extension to the indefinitude of forms, all differentiating themselves, as we have just shown, starting from the original spherical form. From the physical point of view, movement is the necessary factor in all differentiation, and thus the condition of all formal manifestations, and also, simultaneously, of all vital manifestations, both in the domain considered, being equally subject to time and space, and presupposing, on the other hand, a material 'substratum' on which this activity is physically exercised through movement. It is important to note that every corporeal form is necessarily living, since life

36. But this polarization remains potential (therefore wholly ideal, and not perceptible) as long as we do not have to envisage the actual complementarism of fire and water (each of the latter remaining likewise potentially polarized); till then, the two aspects active and passive, can be dissociated only conceptually, since air is still a neutral element.

37. For every point in extension, the static aspect is reflected in relation to the dynamic aspect, which latter is direct as long as it participates immediately in the essence of the principial point (implying an identification), but which in its indivisible unity, however, is itself reflected in relation to this point considered in itself. One must never lose sight of the fact that the consideration of activity and passivity implies only a relation or a link between two terms envisaged as mutually complementary.

as well as form is a condition of all physical existence.[38] Moreover, this physical life consists of an indefinitude of degrees, its most general divisions corresponding to the three kingdoms mineral, vegetable, and animal, at least from our terrestrial point of view, but without the distinctions between these kingdoms having more than a wholly relative value.[39] It follows that in this domain any form is always in a state of movement or activity, manifesting the life proper to it, and that it can be envisaged statically, that is to say at rest, only through a conceptual abstraction.[40]

It is through mobility that form manifests itself physically and is rendered perceptible to us, and, just as mobility is the characteristic nature of air (*vāyu*), touch is the sense which corresponds properly to form, for it is by touch that we generally perceive form. But owing to its limited mode of perception which operates exclusively

38. Conversely, it is clearly understood thereby that in the physical world life cannot manifest itself otherwise than in forms; but this is no proof against the possible existence of a non-formal life outside of this physical world, without it being legitimate however to consider life itself, in all the indefinitude of its extension, as being more than a contingent possibility comparable to all the others, and in the same way as the others, arising in the determination of certain individual states of manifested beings, states which proceed from certain specialized and refracted aspects of Universal Being.

39. It is impossible to determine characteristics that permit the establishment of certain and precise distinctions between these three kingdoms, which seem closely akin, especially in their most elementary forms, which are in some way embryonic.

40. From this it is sufficiently clear what, from the physical point of view, one should think of the so-called 'principle of inertia of matter': truly inert matter, that is to say matter deprived of all attribution or actual property, and therefore indistinct and undifferentiated; a pure passive and receptive power on which is exercised an activity of which it is not the cause, is, we repeat, only conceivable when envisaged apart from this activity of which it is only the 'substratum' and from which it takes all its reality. It is this activity (to which it is not opposed, in order to furnish a support for it, except by the effect of a contingent reflection which does not give to it any independent reality) which, through reaction (by reason of this very reflection), in fact, in the special conditions of physical existence, makes of it the place of all sensory phenomena (just like other phenomena which do not reappear within the limits of our sense perception), the substantial and plastic milieu of all corporeal modifications.

through contact,[41] this sense still cannot directly and immediately give us the full idea of corporeal extension in three dimensions,[42] which belongs only to the sense of sight; but here the actual existence of this extension is already assumed through that of form, since it conditions the manifestation of this latter, at least in the physical world.[43]

Moreover, insofar as air proceeds from ether, sound is also perceptible therein; since, as we have established above, differentiated movement implies the distinction of the directions of space, the role of air in the perception of sound, apart from its quality of medium in which the etheric vibrations are amplified, will consist principally in enabling us to recognize the direction according to which this sound is produced in relation to the actual situation of our body. In the physiological organs of hearing, the part corresponding to this perception of direction (a perception which, moreover, effectively becomes complete only with and through the notion of extension in three dimensions) constitutes what are known as the 'semi-circular canals', which are precisely oriented according to the three dimensions of physical space.[44]

Finally, to a point of view other than that of the perceptible qualities, air is the substantial medium whence the vital breath (*prāna*) proceeds. This is why the five phases of respiration and assimilation, which are modalities or aspects of *prāna*, are identified as a whole with *vāyu*. This is the particular role of air with regard to life; hence

41. In this connection it must be noted that the organs of touch are distributed over the whole surface (exterior and interior) of our organism which finds itself in contact with the atmospheric medium.

42. The contact can only be operated between surfaces by reason of the impenetrability of physical matter (a property to which we shall return later), so that the resulting perception can therefore give, in an immediate way, only the notion of surface, in which just two dimensions of extension occur.

43. We always add this restriction so as not to limit in any way the indefinite possibilities for combinations of the various contingent conditions of existence, and in particular those of corporeal existence, which are found to be united in a necessarily constant way only in the domain of this special modality.

44. This explains why it is said that the directions of space are the ears of *Vaishvānara*.

we see that, just as we had foreseen for this element as for ether, we have really had to consider the totality of the five conditions of corporeal existence and their relations. The same will hold true for each of the other three elements, which proceed from the first two, and which we shall now discuss.[45]

45. [The text ends here. Ed.]

SOME MODERN ERRORS

1

THE 'EMPIRICISM' OF THE ANCIENTS

ON NUMEROUS OCCASIONS we have already explained the fundamental difference between the sciences of the ancients and the moderns, which is that between traditional and profane sciences; but this is a question involving so many commonly held errors that it cannot be overemphasized. Thus it is often affirmed as self-evident that the science of the ancients was purely 'empirical', which basically amounts to saying that it was not really even a science strictly speaking, but only a kind of practical and utilitarian knowledge. Now it is easy to see on the contrary that preoccupations of this order have never held such sway as among the moderns, and also, even without going further back than what is called 'classical' antiquity, that everything concerned with experimentation was considered by the ancients as only constituting knowledge of a very inferior degree. It is not very clear how all of this can be reconciled with the preceding affirmation; and, by a remarkable inconsistency, those very people who express the latter almost never fail to reproach the ancients for their disdain for experimentation!

The source of the error in question, as also for a multitude of others, is the notion of 'evolution' or 'progress': by virtue of the latter, it is claimed that all knowledge began in a rudimentary state from which it was to be gradually raised and developed. A sort of crude, primitive simplicity is postulated which, of course, cannot be the object of any observation; and it is maintained that everything started from below, as if it were not contradictory to accept that the superior can originate in the inferior. Such a concept is not just any error, but quite specifically a 'counter-truth'; by this we mean that it goes right against the grain of the truth by a strange inversion which is very characteristic of the modern spirit. The truth, on the contrary, is that since the beginning there has been a sort of degradation or continual 'descent', going from spirituality to materiality, that is, from the superior to the inferior, and manifesting itself in all the domains of human activity; and from this, in fairly recent times, sprang the profane sciences separated from any transcendent principle and justified solely by the practical applications to which they give rise, for this is in sum all that interests modern man, who cares little for pure knowledge, and who, as we have just said, only attributes his own tendencies[1] to the ancients because he cannot even conceive that theirs may have been altogether different, any more than he can imagine that there may exist sciences altogether different in objective and method from those which he himself cultivates exclusively.

This same error also implies 'empiricism' when understood to designate a philosophical theory, that is, the idea—also very modern—that all knowledge derives entirely from experience and, more precisely, from perceptible experience; in reality, this is only one form of the claim that everything comes from below. It is clear that outside of this preconceived notion there is no reason to suppose that the first state of all knowledge must have been an 'empirical' state; this comparison between the two meanings of the same word certainly has nothing fortuitous about it, and it could be said that it is the philosophical 'empiricism' of the moderns that leads them to attribute to the ancients a *de facto* 'empiricism'. Now it must be admitted that we have never been able to understand even the possibility of such a concept, so much does it seem to us to go against all evidence: that there may be knowledge that does not come from the senses, is, purely and simply, a matter of fact; but the moderns, who claim that they rely only on facts, ignore them or readily deny them when they do not agree with their theories. In short, the existence of this notion of 'empiricism' simply proves that

1. It is by an illusion of the same kind that moderns, because they are driven above all by 'economic' motives, claim to explain all historical events by linking them to causes of this order.

among those who have expressed it and among those who accept it, certain faculties of a supra-sensible order beginning, it goes without saying, with pure intellectual intuition, have entirely disappeared.[2]

Generally speaking, the sciences as understood by the moderns, that is to say the secular sciences, actually assume nothing more or less than a rational elaboration of perceptible data; it is therefore they who are truly 'empirical' as to their point of departure; and it could be said that moderns unduly confuse this starting-point of their sciences with the origin of all science. Yet even in their sciences there are sometimes diminished or altered vestiges of ancient knowledge, the real nature of which escapes them; and here we are thinking especially of the mathematical sciences, the essential concepts of which cannot be drawn from sensory experience. The efforts of certain philosophers to explain 'empirically' the origin of these ideas is at times irresistibly comical! And, if some are tempted to protest when we speak of diminishment or alteration for the worse, we will ask them to compare in this regard, for example, the traditional science of numbers to profane arithmetic; no doubt they will then be able to understand quite easily what is meant.

Moreover, most of the profane sciences really owe their origin only to fragments or even, one could say, to residues from misunderstood traditional sciences: elsewhere we have mentioned as particularly characteristic the example of chemistry, which arose, not from genuine alchemy, but from its denaturation by 'puffers', that is, by the profane who, ignorant of the true meaning of hermetic symbols, understood them in a crudely literal sense. We have also cited the case of astronomy, which represents only the material portion of ancient astrology, isolated from everything that constituted the 'spirit' of this science, and irremediably lost to moderns, who go off spouting foolishly that astronomy was discovered in a totally 'empirical' way by Chaldean shepherds, without suspecting that the

2. Disappearance of these faculties as to their effective exercise, of course, for in spite of everything they subsist in the latent state in every human being; but this kind of atrophy can reach such a degree that their manifestation becomes completely impossible, and this is indeed what we notice in the great majority of our contemporaries.

name 'Chaldean' was really the designation of a priestly caste! We could multiply examples of the same kind to establish a comparison between sacred cosmogonies and the theory of the 'nebula' and other similar hypotheses, or, in another order of ideas, to show the degeneration of medicine from its ancient dignity of 'sacerdotal art', and so on. The conclusion would always be the same: secular people, having illegitimately taken over fragments of knowledge of which they can grasp neither the scope nor the significance, have formed so-called independent sciences which are worth just exactly what they themselves are worth; and thus modern science, which has sprung from them, is literally only the science of the ignorant.[3]

The traditional sciences, as we have so often said, are characterized essentially by their attachment to transcendent principles, upon which they depend strictly as more or less contingent applications, and this is the complete contrary of 'empiricism'; but the principles necessarily escape the profane, and that is why the latter, even our modern experts, can never really be other than 'empirical'. Since the time when, as a result of the degradation alluded to previously, men have no longer been equally qualified for all knowledge, that is to say, at least since the beginning of the *Kali-Yuga*, the profane became inevitable. However, in order that their truncated and falsified science be taken seriously and pass for what it is not, it was necessary that true knowledge together with the initiatic organizations which were charged with conserving and transmitting it disappear, and this is precisely what has happened in the Western world in the course of the last centuries.

We should add that in the way moderns envisage the knowledge of the ancients one may clearly see this negation of any 'suprahuman' element which constitutes the basis of the anti-traditional spirit, and which, after all, is only a direct result of secular ignorance. Not only is everything reduced to purely human proportions, but, as a result of this reversal of all things which the 'evolutionist' conception entails, they go so far as to put the 'infra-human' at the

3. By a curious irony, the 'scientism' of our time insists above all upon proclaiming itself 'secular', without being aware that this is, quite simply, the explicit avowal of that ignorance.

origin. What is most serious is that in the eyes of our contemporaries these things seem to be self-evident; because they no longer even have any inkling that things might be otherwise, they go so far as to state them as if they could not even be disputed, and to present as 'facts' the most unfounded hypotheses. This is most serious, we say, because it is what makes us fear that, having reached such a point, the deviation of the modern spirit may be altogether irremediable.

These considerations will help us understand why it is absolutely futile to seek to establish any accord or reconciliation whatsoever between traditional and secular knowledge, and why the first does not have to ask of the second a 'confirmation' of which it has no need in and of itself. If we stress this, it is because we know how widespread this point of view is today among those who have some idea of traditional doctrines; yet an 'exterior' idea, so to speak, is insufficient to enable one to penetrate their profound nature, as well as to prevent one from being deluded by the false prestige of modern science and its practical applications. The former, by thus putting on the same plane things that are in no way comparable, not only waste their time and effort, but also risk going astray and misleading others into all kinds of false conceptions. And the many varieties of 'occultism' are there to show that this danger is only too real.

2

THE DIFFUSION OF KNOWLEDGE AND THE MODERN SPIRIT

We have already had more than one occasion to say what we think of the modern tendencies to 'propaganda' and 'popularization', and of the incomprehension of true knowledge that they imply; so we do not intend to return yet again to the many disadvantages presented generally by the unconsidered diffusion of an 'education' which is intended to be distributed equally to everyone under forms and by methods that are identical, and that can only result in a kind of levelling; here, as everywhere in our time, quality is sacrificed to quantity. Yet in a relative way this kind of activity is perhaps excusable in light of the very character of the secular education in question, which offers no knowledge in the true sense of the word, and contains absolutely nothing of a profound order. What makes it especially harmful is that it is taken for what it is not and tends to deny everything that is beyond itself, thus stifling all possibilities relating to a higher domain. But what is perhaps more serious still—and what we wish especially to call attention to here—is that some people believe they are able to expound traditional doctrines on the model as it were of this same profane education, applying considerations that take no account of the actual nature of these doctrines, and of the essential differences that exist between them and everything that is today designated by the terms 'science' and 'philosophy'. Here we see the modern spirit penetrating even into what is by very definition radically opposed, so that it is not difficult to understand what destructive consequences, may result from it, consequences unknown even to those who often in good faith and with no precise intention make themselves the instruments of such penetration.

We have recently had an example of this which is rather surprising in more than one respect: one cannot stifle a certain astonishment in hearing it asserted first of all that 'in India it has long been believed that certain aspects of the Vedantic teaching must be kept secret,' that 'the popularization of certain truths was reputed to be dangerous,' and that 'one was even forbidden to speak of it outside a small circle of initiates.' There is no call to cite any names here, since this case is of value only to 'illustrate' a certain mentality; but to account for our astonishment we must at least say that these assertions do not come from an orientalist or Theosophist, but from a native Hindu. Now, if there was ever a country where it has always been held that the theoretical aspect of doctrine (for of course there is no question here, of 'realization' and its proper means) could be expounded with no other reservation than that of their ultimate inexpressibility, it is precisely India. Given the actual constitution of traditional Hindu organization, one cannot imagine who could be qualified to prohibit anyone's speaking of this or that; in fact, such a situation can only occur where there is a clear distinction between esoterism and exoterism, which is not the case for India. Neither one say that the 'popularization' of doctrines is dangerous, but rather that, were it even possible, it would simply be useless, since in reality truths of this order resist all 'popularization' by their very nature. However clearly they may be presented, they will be understood only by those qualified to understand them, while for the rest the doctrines will be as if they do not exist. Our opinion of the 'secrets' so dear to pseudo-esoterists is known well enough: a reserve in the theoretical order can only be justified by considerations of simple expediency and thus on purely contingent grounds; ultimately, any outward secret can only have the value of a symbol, or sometimes also that of a 'discipline', which would not be without benefit... But the modern mentality is such that it cannot abide any secret or even any reserve; the import and significance of such things entirely escape it, and its incomprehension in their regard quite naturally engenders hostility; yet the truly monstrous character of a world in which everything would be made 'public' (we say 'would' for in spite of everything we have not yet come to such a pass) is such that it would merit a special study in itself. But this is not the moment to indulge in perhaps too facile 'anticipations', and we will simply say that we can only pity those who have fallen so low as to be able to live, literally as well as symbolically, in 'hives of glass'.

But to continue with our citations: 'Today, one can no longer take these restrictions into account; the average level of culture has been raised and minds have been prepared to receive the complete teaching.' Here we see as clearly as possible the confusion of traditional teaching with profane education, designated by the term 'culture', which in our time has come to be one of its standard designations. But this is something that has not the least connection to traditional teaching or to the aptitude for receiving it; and in addition, since the so-called raising of the 'average level' has its inevitable counterpart in the disappearance of the intellectual elite, one can truly say that this 'culture' represents exactly the opposite of the preparation in question here. We wonder moreover how a Hindu can completely ignore our present position in the *Kali-Yuga*, and can go so far as to say that 'the time has come when the entire system of the *Vedānta* can be publicly expounded,' whereas the least knowledge of cyclical laws obliges one to say, on the contrary, that they are less favorable than ever; and if it has never been 'within the reach of the common man,' for whom it is not made, it certainly is not so today, for this 'common man' has never been so totally lacking in understanding. Besides, the truth is that for this very reason everything representing traditional knowledge of a truly profound order, and thus corresponding to what an 'integral teaching' must imply, is made increasingly difficult of access—and this everywhere. Faced with the invasive modern and profane spirit, it is all too obvious that it could not be otherwise; how then can one so misunderstand the reality as to affirm its complete opposite, and this with as much tranquillity as if one were expressing the most incontestable of truths?

The reasons our author advances for his current interest in spreading the *Vedāntic* teaching are no less extraordinary. First, he highlights the 'development of social ideas and political institutions'; but even if there truly is a 'development' (and in any case he should specify what sense he intends), this is still something that has no more relation to the understanding of a metaphysical doctrine than has the diffusion of secular education. Moreover, it is enough to observe in any country of the East how political preoccupations hinder the knowledge of traditional truths wherever they have been introduced, for one to think it more justifiable to speak of an incompatibility (more or less of fact) than of a possible agreement between two such 'developments'. We do not really see what connection 'social life', in the purely profane sense as conceived by the moderns, could possibly have with spirituality; on the other hand, there was such a connection when social life was integrated into a traditional civilization. But it is precisely the modern spirit that has destroyed such civilizations, or aims to destroy them wherever they still exist; that being so, what can one really expect from a 'development' the most characteristic trait of which is its opposition to all spirituality?

But he invokes yet another reason: 'Furthermore, for the *Vedānta* as for the truths of science, a scientific secrecy no longer exists today; science does not hesitate to publish the most recent discoveries.' In fact, this profane science is made only for the 'general public', and this is indeed its whole raison d'être; it is all too evident that science is really nothing more than it appears to be, since—we cannot say 'in principle', but rather 'in the absence of principle'—it restricts itself to the surface of things. Surely there is nothing in it worth the trouble to keep secret, or, to speak more precisely, that merits being reserved for the use of an elite; and besides, only an elite need do such a thing. What assimilation, then, can one possibly want to establish between the so-called truths of profane science and the teachings of a doctrine such as the *Vedānta*? It is always the same confusion, and one may well wonder just how deeply someone who commends it so insistently can understand the doctrine that he wishes to teach; in any event, assertions of this kind can only prevent this comprehension in those to whom it is addressed. Between the traditional spirit and the modern spirit there really can be no accommodation; every concession made to the second is necessarily at the expense of the first, and can only result in a weakening of the doctrine, even when its consequences do not go as far as their most extreme and also most logical outcome, that is, to the point of true deformation.

It will be noted that in all this we do not adopt a point of view that includes the hypothetical dangers that a general diffusion of true knowledge could present; we only affirm the pure and simple impossibility of such a diffusion, especially in present conditions, for the world has never been further from true knowledge than it is today. If, however, one insists on speaking of dangers, we will say this: formerly, in explaining doctrinal truths exactly as they are, and without any 'popularization', one sometimes risked being misunderstood, but now the risk is simply that of not being understood at all, which perhaps is in fact less serious in a certain sense, although we do not really see what the partisans of diffusion have to gain thereby.

3

THE SUPERSTITION OF 'VALUE'

In certain of our works we have denounced a number of specifically modern 'superstitions', the most striking characteristic of which is that ultimately they rest only on the prestige attributed to a word, a prestige all the greater as the idea evoked by this word is, for most people, the more vague and inconsistent. The influence exercised by such words themselves, independently of what they express or should express, has in fact never been as great as in our time. It is like a caricature of the power inherent in ritual formulas, and those who are most intent on denying the latter are also, through a singular 'backlash', the first to allow themselves to adopt what is actually a kind of profane parody. It goes without saying that this power of formulas or words is not at all of the same order in the two instances: the power of ritual formulas, which is essentially based on 'sacred science', is something fully effective, and is truly operative in the most diverse domains, according to the effects one wishes to obtain; on the contrary, that of their profane counterfeit is naturally only capable—at least directly—of a purely 'psychological' and above all sentimental action, that is, it falls within the most illusory of all domains. This is not to say that such an action is harmless; far from it, for these 'subjective' illusions, however insignificant they may be in themselves, nevertheless have very real consequences in all human activity; and, above all, they contribute greatly to the destruction of all true intellectuality, which moreover is probably the chief function assigned them in the 'plan' of the modern subversion.

The superstitions of which we speak vary to some extent from moment to moment, for in all of this there is a kind of 'fashion', as with all things in our time. We do not mean that when a superstition arises, it at once entirely replaces the others, for on the contrary we can easily observe their coexistence in the contemporary mentality; but at least the most recent takes a predominant place and relegates the others more or less to the background. Thus, keeping more specifically to what we presently have in view, it can be said that there was first the superstition of 'reason', which reached its culmination near the end of the eighteenth century, then the superstitions of 'science' and 'progress', closely attached to the former, but more particularly characteristic of the nineteenth century; more recently still, we see the appearance of the superstition of 'life', which had great success in the early years of the present century. As everything changes with an ever increasing speed, these superstitions, like all the scientific and philosophical theories to which they are linked in a certain way, seem to 'wear out' more and more rapidly. Thus we must now note the emergence of yet another superstition, that of 'value', which apparently only dates from a few years back, but which is already tending to follow in the steps of those that have preceded it.

We are certainly not inclined to exaggerate the importance of philosophy, and above all of modern philosophy, for while recognizing that it may be one of the factors that act more or less on the general mentality, we think that it is far from the most important, and that, under its 'systematic' form, it even represents more of an effect than a cause. As such, however, it expresses in a more clearly defined way what already existed in a diffused state in this mentality, and consequently, in somewhat the same way as a magnifying instrument, it reveals things that could otherwise escape the attention of the observer, or that would be at least more difficult to discern. Also, in order to understand fully what is involved, it helps to recall first of all the stages of the gradual decline of modern philosophical conceptions, which we have already pointed out elsewhere: first, the reduction of all things to the 'human' and to the 'rational'; then the increasingly narrow meaning given to the 'rational' itself, which in the end is envisaged only in its most inferior functions; and finally, a descent into the 'infra-rational' with so-called 'intuitionism' and the various theories that are more or less directly part of it. The 'rationalists' at least still spoke of 'truth', although for them it could obviously only be a question of a very relative truth; the 'intuitionists' tried to replace the 'true' with the 'real', which could be almost the same thing if one kept to the normal meaning of words, but which is very far from being the case in fact, for here one must take into account the strange deformation by which, in current usage, the word 'reality' has come to designate exclusively things of the sensible order, which is to say precisely those that have the least degree of reality. Next, the 'pragmatists' chose to ignore truth entirely, and to suppress it in a certain manner by substituting for it 'utility'; this is then really the fall into the 'subjective', for it is quite clear that the utility of a thing is by no means a quality that resides in the thing itself, but depends entirely on the one who appraises it and who makes it the object of a kind of individual appreciation, without in the least concerning himself with what the thing is outside of this appreciation, that is to say with all that it really is. Assuredly, it would be difficult to proceed any further on the path of the negation of all intellectuality.

The 'intuitionists' and the 'pragmatists', and likewise the representatives of some other related schools of lesser importance, willingly adorn their theories with the label 'philosophy of life'; but it seems that already this expression no longer enjoys as much success as it once did, and that today it is the 'philosophy of values' that is most in favor. This new philosophy appears to attack the 'real' itself, however one wishes to understand it, almost as 'pragmatism' attacks the 'true'; its affinity in certain respects with 'pragmatism' is obvious, for both 'value' and 'utility' can be no more than a simple matter of individual appreciation, and its 'subjective' character is perhaps even more accentuated, as will be made evident below. It is possible that the current success of the word 'value' is due in part to the rather grossly material sense that, although not inherent to its original meaning, is associated with it in ordinary language: when one speaks of 'value' or 'evaluation', one immediately thinks of something that can be 'counted' or 'numbered', and it must be agreed that this accords quite well with the 'quantitative' spirit characteristic of the modern world. However, this is at most only half of the explanation; indeed, it must be remembered that 'pragmatism', which is defined by the fact that it relates everything to 'action', does not only mean 'utility' in a material sense, but also in a moral sense. 'Value' is equally subject to these two meanings, although the second clearly predominates in the conception in question, for the moral—or more exactly 'moralist'—aspect is still exaggerated. This 'philosophy of values' appears above all as a form of 'idealism', and this no doubt explains its hostility toward the 'real', since it is understood that in the special language of modern philosophers, 'idealism' is opposed to 'realism'.

It is known that for the most part modern philosophy thrives on ambiguity, and there is something noteworthy hidden in this label 'idealism'. The word can in fact be derived both from 'idea' and from 'ideal'; and in fact, the two essential characteristics that can easily be discerned in the 'philosophy of values' correspond to this twin derivation. 'Idea' is of course taken here in the purely 'psychological' sense, which is the only sense the moderns know (and it will be seen shortly that it is useful to emphasize this point in order to dispel yet another ambiguity), and this is the 'subjectivist' side of the conception in question; as to the 'ideal', it represents no less obviously its 'moralist' side. Thus, in this case the two meanings of 'idealism' are closely associated and as it were support each other, because they both correspond to rather general tendencies of the contemporary mentality: 'psychologism' indicates a state of mind that is far from being peculiar to 'professional' philosophers, and furthermore, the fascination which the empty word 'ideal' has exercised on most of our contemporaries is only too well known!

What is almost incredible is that the philosophy in question claims to have its roots in 'Platonic idealism'; and it is difficult to refrain from a certain stupefaction in seeing the assertion that 'true reality lies not in the object but in the idea, that is to say in an act of thought,' attributed to Plato. First, there is no 'Platonic idealism' in any of the meanings that the moderns give to the word 'idealism'; for Plato, 'ideas' are neither 'psychological' nor 'subjective', and have absolutely nothing in common with an 'act of thought'; on the contrary, they are the transcendent principles or 'archetypes' of all things. That is why they constitute reality par excellence, and although Plato himself did not express it in this way (any more than he anywhere expressly formulates something that could be called a 'theory of ideas'), one could say that the 'world of ideas' is ultimately nothing other that the 'Divine Intellect'; what connection can this have with the product of an individual 'thought'? Even from the mere point of view of the 'history of philosophy', there is a truly extraordinary error here; and not only is Plato neither 'idealist' nor 'subjectivist' in any degree, but it would be impossible to be more completely 'realist' than he; it is surely more than paradoxical that the avowed enemies of the 'real' wish to make him their predecessor. Furthermore, these same philosophers commit yet another error that is hardly less serious when, in trying to connect their 'moralism' to Plato, they invoke the 'central' role, as it were, that he assigns to the 'idea of the Good'; here, to use Scholastic terminology, we can say that they quite simply confuse the 'transcendental Good' with the 'moral good', so great is their ignorance of certain notions, no matter how elementary. When one sees the moderns thus 'interpret' ancient conceptions—even though no more than philosophy is involved—can one still be astonished how outrageously they deform doctrines of a more profound order?

The truth is that the 'philosophy of values' cannot claim the least connection with any ancient doctrine whatsoever, save in indulging in very poor puns on the 'ideas' and the 'good', to which must be added yet other confusions—and rather common ones—such as that of 'spirit' with 'mind'; on the contrary, it is one of the most typically modern confusions, arising from the 'subjectivist' and 'moralist' traits noted above. It is not difficult to understand at what point it is thereby opposed to the traditional spirit, as is all 'idealism' moreover, the logical outcome of which is to make truth itself (and today one would also say the 'real') dependent on the operations of individual 'thought'. At a time when intellectual disorder had not yet reached the point it has today, perhaps certain 'idealists' sometimes retreated before the enormity of such a consequence, but we do not believe that contemporary philosophers have such reservations... But after all this, one may still wonder just what exactly is served by promoting this particular idea of 'value', thrust thus into the world like a new 'slogan' or, if one wishes, a new 'suggestion'. The answer to this question is also easy, if we simply consider that nearly the entire modern deviation could be described as a series of substitutions that amount to just so many falsifications in all orders. It is in fact easier to destroy a thing by claiming to replace it, even with a more or less crude parody, than to acknowledge openly that one wishes to leave behind only nothingness; and, even when it is a question of a thing that already no longer in fact exists, one can still have an interest in devising an imitation in order to prevent anyone from feeling the need to restore it, or in order to create an obstacle for those who might in fact have such an intention. Thus, to take only one or two examples of the first case, the idea of 'free enquiry' was invented in order to destroy spiritual authority, not by denying it purely and simply all at once, but by substituting for it a false authority, that of individual reason; or again, philosophical 'rationalism' made a point of replacing intellectuality with what is only a caricature. For us, the idea of 'value' seems to be connected rather to the second case; it is already a long time since anyone has in fact recognized any real hierarchy, that is, one founded essentially on the very nature of things. For one reason or another—a point we do not intend to investigate here—it seemed opportune (doubtless not to the philosophers, for in all likelihood they were merely the first dupes) to establish in the public mentality a false hierarchy based solely on sentimental appreciation, and hence entirely 'subjective' (and all the more innocuous, from the point of view of modern 'egalitarianism', which finds itself thus consigned to the mists of the 'ideal', or, one might say, to the fancies of the imagination). One could say, in sum, that 'values' represent a counterfeit of hierarchy used by a world that has been led to the negation of all true hierarchy.

What is even less reassuring is that some dare to qualify these 'values' as 'spiritual', and the abuse of this word is no less significant than all the rest. In fact, here we recognize another counterfeit, that of 'spirituality', the different forms of which we have already denounced; would the 'philosophy of values' also have some role to play in this connection? What in any case is not in doubt is that we are no longer at the stage where 'materialism' and 'positivism' exert a preponderant influence; henceforth it is a question of something else, which, to fulfill its purpose, must assume a more subtle character; and, to state clearly our complete thought on this point, in the order of philosophical ideas, and by means of their reactions on the general mentality, 'idealism' and 'subjectivism' at present are and no doubt will increasingly be the principal obstacles to a full restoration of true intellectuality.

4

THE SENSE OF PROPORTIONS

IN WITNESSING the confusion reigning in our time in every domain, we have often emphasized that, in order to escape it, one needs to know above all how to put each thing in its place, that is, to situate it with respect to other things exactly according to its own nature and exact importance. Most of our contemporaries in fact no longer know how to do this because they no longer have an idea of any true hierarchy; this idea, which in a way is part of the foundation of every traditional civilization, is for this same reason an idea which the forces of subversion, whose action has produced what is called the modern spirit, try especially to destroy. Thus, mental disorder today exists everywhere, even among those who call themselves 'traditionalists' (and we have already shown how what this word implies is not sufficient to react effectively against this state of things); in particular, the sense of proportions is strangely lacking, to the point that one not only sees what is most contingent or even most insignificant taken for the essential, but even the normal and abnormal, the lawful and unlawful, are put on equal footing, as if both were equivalent and had the same right to exist.

A characteristic example of this mentality is furnished by a 'neo-Thomist' philosopher[1] who in a recent article stated that in 'the

1. In order to avoid any ambiguity and any dispute, let us explain that by 'neo-Thomist' we mean an attempt to 'adapt' Thomism; this implies rather serious concessions to modernist ideas which sometimes affect much more than one might think even those who readily proclaim themselves 'anti-modern'; our age is full of such contradictions.

sacred type of civilization' (we would rather say 'traditional') like the Islamic civilization or the Christian civilization of the Middle Ages, 'the idea of a holy war could have a meaning' but that it 'loses all meaning' in 'the profane type of civilization' such as ours today, 'in which the temporal is more completely distinguished from the spiritual, and, since from now on it is wholly autonomous, it no longer has an instrumental role with regard to the sacred.' Does not this way of speaking seem to indicate that fundamentally one is not far from seeing 'progress' therein, or at least that it is considered something more or less definitively established and from which there is 'from now on' no turning back? Moreover, we would like someone to cite at least one other example of a 'profane type of civilization', because for our part we know of none outside of modern civilization, which, precisely because it is such, is strictly nothing but an anomaly; the plural seems to have been put there expressly to allow a parallel or, as we will explain shortly, an equivalence between this 'profane type' and the 'sacral' or traditional type, which is the type of every normal civilization without exception.

It goes without saying that this is not a mere recognition of a state of fact, which would raise no objection; but from such a recognition to the acceptance of this state as constituting a lawful form of civilization in the same way as that form which it negates, there is a veritable abyss. That one should say that the ideal of 'holy war' is inapplicable in present circumstances is a fact that is only too obvious, and one with which everyone will necessarily agree; but let no one say because of this that the idea has no more meaning, for the 'intrinsic value of an idea', especially a traditional idea like this, is entirely independent of contingencies and has not the least connection with what is called 'historical reality', for it belongs to a completely different order of reality. To make the value of an idea—that is, ultimately, its very truth, for as soon as it is a question of an idea we do not see how its value could be anything else—depend on the vicissitudes of human events is the very mark of that 'historicism' which we have denounced as error on other occasions and which is nothing but one of the forms of modern 'relativism'. That a 'traditionalist' philosopher should share this way of seeing things is indeed regrettably significant! And if, instead of seeing the profane point of view as the degeneration or deviation that it really is, he accords it the same validity as the traditional point of view, how can he then object to the too well known 'tolerance', also a specifically modern and profane attitude, that consists in giving every error the same rights as the truth?

We have dwelt at some length on this example because it is very representative of a certain mentality; but one could of course find a great many others from a more or less closely related order of ideas. The undue importance attributed to the profane sciences by the more or less authorized (but quite poorly qualified) representatives of traditional doctrines, ultimately belong to the same tendencies. Indeed, an attempt is constantly made to accommodate the doctrines to the more or less hypothetical and always provisional results of these sciences, as if between the one and the other there could be any common measure, and as if they were things situated on the same level. Among those who believe themselves obliged to adopt it, a similar attitude, its weakness particularly visible in religious 'apologetics', shows a truly singular misunderstanding of the value—we would even willingly say of the dignity—of the doctrines they think they are thus defending, while in fact they only abase and diminish them. These same people are thereby led imperceptibly and unwittingly to the worst compromises, thus offering a bowed head to the noose held out to them by those who seek only to destroy all that has a traditional character and who know very well what they are about in leading them onto this terrain of useless profane discussion. It is only by maintaining the transcendence of tradition in an absolute way that one makes (or rather keeps) it inaccessible to every attack by its enemies, whom one must never consent to treat as 'adversaries'; but in the absence of the sense of proportions and of hierarchy, who still understands this today?

We have just spoken of concessions made to the scientific point of view in the sense that this latter is understood by the modern world; but the too frequent illusions about the value and scope of the philosophical point of view also imply the same kind of error of perspective since by very definition this point of view is no less profane than the other. One should be content to smile at the pretensions of those who wish to put purely human 'systems', products of mere individual thought, in parallel or in opposition to traditional doctrines, which are essentially supra-human, if in so many cases they did not succeed only too well in having these pretensions taken seriously. If the consequences are perhaps less serious, it is only because philosophy has a more restricted influence than profane science does on the general mentality of our time. Nevertheless, here too it would be a great mistake to conclude that the danger is non-existent or negligible just because it does not appear to be as immediate. Moreover, even when in this regard there is no other result than to 'neutralize' the efforts of many 'traditionalists' by leading them into a domain where there is no real headway to be made regarding a restoration of the traditional spirit, this is still always so much the more gain for the enemy. Our reflections on another occasion concerning various illusions of the political or social order also find an application in such cases.

From this philosophical point of view, let it be said in passing, it sometimes happens that things take a rather amusing turn; we are speaking of the 'reactions' of certain 'polemicists' of this kind when they find themselves on that rare occasion in the presence of someone who positively refuses to follow them onto this terrain, and of the amazement mingled with vexation, even rage, that they exhibit in realizing that their whole argument falls into the void, something to which they are as little able to resign themselves as they are obviously incapable of understanding the reasons. We have even dealt with people who claimed we were obliged to bestow on the flimsy constructions of their individual fantasies a significance that we must reserve exclusively for traditional truths alone; naturally we could only demur, hence the fit of truly indescribable anger; thus it is no longer only the sense of proportions that is lacking but also the sense of the ridiculous.

But let us return to more serious things. Since these are errors of perspective we will point out another, which is to tell the truth of a wholly different order, for it occurs in the traditional domain itself and is ultimately only a particular case of the difficulty men generally have in admitting whatever surpasses their own point of view. That some, even the great majority, should have their horizon limited to a single traditional form or even to a certain aspect of this form, and that they should consequently be enclosed in a point of view that could be called more or less narrowly 'local', is something perfectly legitimate in itself and in any case wholly inevitable; but on the other hand what is in no way acceptable is that they should imagine that this same point of view with all its inherent limitations must also belong to everyone without exception, including those who are conscious of the essential unity of all traditions. Against anyone who manifests such an incomprehension we must steadfastly maintain the rights of those who have risen to a higher level from which the perspective is necessarily wholly different; that they give the benefit of the doubt to what they themselves, at least presently, are unable to understand, and that they not meddle with anything beyond their competence—this is basically all we ask of them. Moreover, we very readily recognize that for them this limited point of view is not without certain advantages, first because it permits them to cling intellectually to something rather simple and to be satisfied with it, and then, because of the 'local' situation to which they are restricted, they certainly bother no one, which avoids their provoking hostile forces against themselves which, for them, would probably be impossible to resist.

5

THE ORIGINS OF MORMONISM

AMONG THE RELIGIOUS OR PSEUDO-RELIGIOUS sects widespread in America, the Mormon sect is assuredly one of the oldest and most important, and we believe that it would not be without some interest to look at its origins.

At the beginning of the nineteenth century there lived in New England a Presbyterian pastor named Solomon Spalding, who had abandoned his ministry in favor of commerce, where it was not long before he went bankrupt. After this setback, he began writing a kind of novel in biblical style which he entitled *Manuscript Found*, and which, it seems, he counted on to restore his fortune; in this he was mistaken, as he died before he could find a publisher. The subject of this book concerns the history of the North American Indians, who were portrayed as the descendants of the Patriarch Joseph; it was a protracted account of their wars and their supposed migrations from the time of Sedecias, king of Judah, up to the fifth century AD. This account was supposed to have been written by various chroniclers, the last of whom, named Mormon, is said to have deposited it in an underground hiding place.

How had Spalding struck upon the idea of compiling this extremely boring, incredibly monotonous work written in a deplorable style? It is hardly possible to say, and one wonders whether this idea came to him spontaneously or was suggested to him by someone or other, for he is far from having been alone in searching for what had become of the ten lost tribes of Israel and in the attempt to resolve the problem in his own way. We know that some tried to find traces of these tribes in England, and that there are even Englishmen who stoutly claim the honor of this origin for their nation; others sought these same tribes much further afield—as far even as Japan. What is certain is that there are very old Jewish colonies in some regions of the East, notably Cochin in southern India, and also China, which claim to have been established there since the time of the Babylonian captivity. The idea of a migration to America seems much more unlikely and moreover has occurred to others than Spalding; in fact there is a rather remarkable coincidence to be noted here. In 1825, a Jew of Portuguese origin, Mordecaï Manuel Noah, former consul of the United States in Tunis, bought an island named Grand Island situated in the Niagara river, and issued a proclamation urging all his co-religionists to come and settle on this island, which he named Ararat. On September 2nd of the same year, the foundation of the new city was celebrated with great pomp; now, and this is what we wish to draw attention to, the Indians had been invited to send representatives to this ceremony in the capacity of descendants of the lost tribes of Israel, and they also were to find a refuge in the new Ararat. This project came to nothing, and the town was never built. About twenty years later, Noah wrote a book in which he advocated the re-establishment of the Jewish nation in Palestine, and, although his name may be almost forgotten today, he must be regarded as the real promoter of Zionism. The episode that we have cited took place almost five years prior to the foundation of Mormonism; Spalding was already dead, and we do not think that Noah had known of his *Manuscript Found*. In any case, at that point the extraordinary fortune that was reserved for this work could hardly have been foreseen, and Spalding himself probably never suspected that the day would come when the multitudes would consider it a new divine revelation. At this period no one had yet formed the premeditated intention of composing so-called 'inspired' writings such as the *Oahspe Bible* or the *Aquarian Gospel*—wild imaginings which find among the Americans of this day and age a milieu well-prepared to receive them.

In Palmyra, Vermont there was a young man of rather bad reputation named Joseph Smith. He had first attracted the attention of his fellow citizens during one of those periods of religious enthusiasm that the Americans call *revivals*, by spreading the account of a vision with which he claimed to have been favored; after that he became a 'treasure hunter', living on money given to him by the credulous people whom, thanks to certain divinatory processes, he promised to lead to riches buried in the ground. It was at this point, twelve years after the death of its author, that he laid his hand on Spalding's manuscript. It is believed that this manuscript was given him by one of his accomplices, Sidney Rigdon, who could have stolen it from a printery where he was serving his apprenticeship. Still, the widow, brother, and former associate of Spalding recognized and formally affirmed the identity of the *Book of Mormon* with the *Manuscript Found*. But the 'treasure seeker' claimed that, guided by an angel, he had pulled this book from the earth where Mormon had buried it, in the form of plates of gold covered with hieroglyphic characters. He added that the angel had also led him to discover two translucent stones—none other than the *Urim* and *Thummin*—which figured on the breast-plate of the High Priest of Israel,[2] the possession of which, bestowing the gift of tongues and the spirit of prophecy, had allowed him to translate the mysterious plates. Ten or so witnesses said they had seen these plates; three of them even asserted that they had also seen the angel, who had then taken away the plates and kept them under his guard. Among the latter was a certain Martin Harris, who despite the opinion of Professor Anthon of New York, to whom he had submitted a sample of the alleged hieroglyphics, and who cautioned Harris against what seemed to him no more than a common hoax, sold his farm to meet the cost of publishing the manuscript. It is to be assumed that Smith had procured some brass plates upon which he inscribed characters borrowed from various alphabets; according to Professor Anthon,[3] they were mainly a mixture of Greek and Hebrew characters, as well as a crude imitation of a Mexican calendar published by Humboldt. It is extremely difficult to say whether those who helped Smith in the early stages were his dupes or accomplices. In the case

2. Exod. 28:30. These two Hebrew words mean 'light' and 'truth'.
3. Letter to Mr Howe, February 17, 1834.

of Harris, whose fortune was seriously compromised by the initial lack of success of the *Book of Mormon*, he did not hesitate to renounce the new faith and to quarrel with Smith. The latter soon had a revelation which charged his followers with his upkeep; then, on the April 6, 1830, another revelation came appointing him prophet of God, with the mission of teaching men a new religion and establishing the *Church of Latter-Day Saints*, which one had to enter through a new baptism. Smith and his associate Cowdery administered this baptism to each other; at the time the Church consisted of only six members, but after a month it numbered about thirty, including Smith's father and brothers. This Church, in short, differed little from the majority of Protestant sects; in the thirty articles of faith which were then drawn up by the founder, there is reason to note only the condemnation of child baptism (article 4), the belief 'that a man can be called to God by prophecy and by the laying on of hands' (article 5), and that miraculous gifts such as 'prophecy, revelation, visions, healing, exorcism, and the interpretation of tongues' are perpetuated in the Church (article 7), the addition of the *Book of Mormon* to the Bible as being the 'word of God' (article 8), and finally the promise 'that God will again reveal great things concerning His Kingdom' (article 9). Let us also mention article 10, couched as follows: 'We believe in the literal gathering of Israel and the restoration of the ten tribes; we believe that Zion will be rebuilt on this continent, that Christ will reign personally on the earth, and that the earth will be renewed and will receive the heavenly glory.' The beginning of this article curiously recalls the projects of Noah; what follows is the expression of a 'millenarism' which is in no way exceptional in Protestant churches, and which, around 1840 in this same region of New England, would also give birth to the 'Seventh Day Adventists'. Finally, Smith wished to reconstitute the organization of the early Church: Apostles, Prophets, Patriarchs, Evangelists, Elders, Deacons, Pastors, and Doctors, plus two hierarchies of pontiffs, one according to the order of Aaron, the other according to the order of Melchizedek.

The first adherents of the new Church were people with very little education, for the most part small farmers or craftsmen; the least ignorant among them was Sidney Rigdon, the one who had probably put Smith in possession of Spalding's manuscript; and who, also by a revelation, was given responsibility for the literary part of the work; and to him is attributed the first part of the book of *Doctrines and Alliances*, published in 1846, and which is as it were the Mormon New Testament. Furthermore, Rigdon did not hesitate to compel the prophet, to whom he had become indispensable, to have another revelation that shared the leadership between them. Meanwhile, the sect began to grow and to make known its existence abroad: the English *Irvingites*,[4] who also believed in the perpetuation of miraculous gifts in the Church, sent a letter to Smith signed by a 'council of pastors' and expressing their sympathy. But Smith's very success made for him enemies who did not hesitate to recall his less than honorable past. And so, from 1831, the prophet judged it prudent to change his residence; from Fayette, in Seneca County, New York, where he had started his Church, he established himself at Kirtland, in Ohio. Then he and Rigdon took a journey of exploration in the regions of the West, and on their return Smith issued a series of revelations ordering the 'Saints' to go to Jackson County in Missouri to build a 'Holy Zion'. Within a few months, twelve hundred faithful responded to this appeal and set about working to clear the land and to erect the 'New Jerusalem'. But the first occupants of the region underwent all sorts of vexations which finally forced them to leave Zion. During this time, Joseph Smith remained in Kirtland where he had founded a business and bank, from whose till—as we learn from his own autobiography—he and his family had an unlimited right to help themselves freely. In 1837 the bank failed, and Smith and Rigdon, threatened with prosecution for fraud, had to flee to their followers in Missouri. Four years had already passed since the latter had been driven out of Zion, but they had retired into neighboring regions, where they had acquired new properties; upon his arrival, Smith told them the hour had come when he was going to 'trample his enemies under his feet.' The Missourians, having learned of his attitude, were infuriated, and hostilities began almost immediately. The Mormons, defeated,

4. A religious sect named after Edward Irving (1792–1834), a deposed Presbyterian minister. Ed.

had to surrender and started to leave the area immediately; the prophet, handed over to the authorities, managed to escape his guards and rejoin his disciples in Illinois. There the 'Saints' began to construct a town, the city of Nauvoo, on the bank of the Mississippi; proselytes arrived, even from Europe, for a mission sent to England in 1837 had resulted in ten thousand baptisms, and a revelation summoned the new converts to hasten to Nauvoo 'with their money, their gold, and their precious stones.' The state of Illinois accorded the city a charter of incorporation; Joseph Smith was made mayor and organized a militia of which he was named general; thenceforth he often made a show of appearing on horseback and in uniform. His military adviser was a certain General Bennett, who had served in the United States army. Bennett had offered his services to Smith in a letter in which, while professing a complete incredulity as to the latter's divine mission, and even treating the Mormon baptism he had received as a 'joyous masquerade', promised the prophet 'a dedicated assistance and the *appearance* of a sincere faith.' The growing prosperity of the faith carried Smith's vanity to such a point that he dared, in 1844, to declare his candidacy for the presidency of the United States.

It was around this time that polygamy was introduced into Mormonism. The revelation authorizing it is dated July 1843, but for a long time it was kept secret and reserved for a small number of initiates. Only after ten years was the practice admitted publicly by the Mormon leaders.[5] Yet despite the efforts that had been made to conceal the revelation, the outcome of it had been known in spite of everything; a body of opposition formed in the very bosom of the sect made its protests known in a journal called *The Expositor*. The partisans of the prophet razed the journal's workroom; the editors fled and denounced Joseph Smith and his brother Hiram to the authorities as disruptive of the public order. A warrant for their arrest was issued, and in order to execute it, the Illinois government

5. The revelation in question was published in the official organ of the sect, *The Millennium Star*, in January 1853. The other revelations that we alluded to above have all been taken from *Doctrines and Alliances*. We have not thought it necessary to show here an exact reference for each.

appealed to the military. Joseph Smith, seeing that he could not resist, judged it prudent to give himself up and together with his brother was locked up in the county jail at Carthage. On July 27, 1844 an armed crowd invaded the jail and fired on the prisoners. Hiram Smith was killed on the spot, and Joseph, trying to escape through the window, misjudged his jump and was dashed against the foot of the wall; he was thirty-nine years old. It is unlikely that the assailants had assembled spontaneously in front of the prison; it is not known by whom they were led or at least influenced, but it is very likely that someone had an interest in causing Joseph Smith's disappearance at the precise moment when he saw all his ambitions being realized.

In any case, if he was undeniably an impostor—although some had tried to present him as a sincere fanatic—it is not certain that he himself had thought up all his impostures. There are too many other more or less similar cases, where the apparent leaders of a movement are often only the instruments of hidden instigators, whom they themselves perhaps do not always know. A man such as Rigdon, for example, could very likely have played an intermediary role between Smith and the likely instigators. The personal ambition that was part of Smith's character, joined to his lack of scruples, could make him suitable for the realization of more or less shadowy plans; but, beyond certain limits, it risked becoming dangerous, and as is usual in such cases, the instrument is broken mercilessly; this is precisely what happened to Smith. We point to these considerations only by way of hypothesis, not wishing to establish any connection; but this is sufficient to show that it is difficult to make a definitive judgment on individuals, and that the search for those truly responsible is much more complicated than those who hold to outer appearances imagine.

AFTER the prophet's death, four claimants, Rigdon, William Smith, Lyman Wight, and Brigham Young, disputed his succession. It was Brigham Young, a former carpenter and president of the 'College of Apostles', who finally prevailed and was proclaimed 'seer, revealer, and president of the Latter-Day Saints'. The sect continued to grow, but it was soon learned that the inhabitants of nine counties were united in the intention of destroying the Mormons. The leaders then decided on a migration *en masse* of their people to a remote and deserted region in High-California belonging to Mexico. This news was announced by a 'catholic epistle' dated January 20, 1846. The Mormons' neighbors agreed to let them go quietly, on condition that they leave before the beginning of the following summer; the 'Saints' took advantage of this delay to complete the temple they were building on the summit of the Nauvoo hill, and to which a revelation had attached various mysterious blessings; the consecration took place in May. The citizens of Illinois, seeing in this a lack of sincerity and the sign of an intention on the part of the Mormons to return, brutally drove from their homes those who were still there and, on September 17, took possession of the abandoned town. The emigrants began a punishing journey; many of them were left by the wayside, and some even died of cold and privations. In spring, the president went on ahead with a body of pioneers; on July 21, 1847, they reached the valley of the Great Salt Lake and, struck by the similarity of its geographic configuration to that of the land of Canaan, resolved to found there a *stake of Zion*, while awaiting the time when they could reconquer the real Zion, that is, the city in Jackson County that Smith's prophecies assured them would be their heritage. When the colony was assembled, they numbered four thousand people. It grew rapidly, and six years later the number of its members had already reached thirty thousand. In 1848, the country had been ceded by Mexico to the United States; the inhabitants asked Congress to establish them as a sovereign state under the name 'State of Deseret', taken from the *Book of Mormon*, but Congress only established the country as a Territory under the name of Utah, which could only become a free State when its population numbered sixty thousand men. This encouraged the Mormons to intensify their propaganda in order to attain this number as quickly as possible and so legalize polygamy and their other particular institutions. In the meantime, the president Brigham Young was named governor of Utah. From this moment, the material prosperity of the Mormons as well as their numbers continued to grow, in spite of some unfortunate episodes, among which may be noted a schism which occurred in 1851. Those who had not followed the emigration formed a 'Reorganized Church' with its center at Lamoni, in Iowa, which claimed to be the only legitimate church. They appointed as their head the prophet's own son, young Joseph Smith, who had been living in Independence, Missouri. According to an official statistic dated 1911, this 'Reorganized Church' then numbered fifty thousand members, while the branch in Utah numbered three hundred and fifty thousand.

THE success of Mormonism may seem astonishing. It is likely that it is due more to the hierarchical and theocratic organization of the sect—very cleverly conceived, it must be acknowledged—than to the value of its doctrine, although the very eccentricity of the latter enabled it to exercise an attraction on certain minds; in America especially, the most absurd things of this kind succeed in an incredible fashion. This doctrine has not remained the same as it was at the beginning, which is easily understood, since new revelations could come along and modify it at any moment. Thus in the *Book of Mormon* polygamy was called an abomination—'an abomination in the eyes of the Lord'—which did not prevent Joseph Smith from receiving another revelation by which it became 'the great blessing of the last Alliance'. The strictly doctrinal innovations seemed to have been due especially to Orson Pratt, under whose intellectual domination Smith had fallen toward the end of his life, and who had a more or less vague knowledge of the ideas of Hegel and some other German philosophers, popularized by writers such as Parker and Emerson.[6]

The religious ideas of the Mormons are the grossest anthropomorphism, as these extracts from one of their catechisms proves:

> QUESTION 28. What is God?—An intelligent and material being, having a body and limbs.
> QUESTION 38. Is he also susceptible to passion?—Yes, he eats, he drinks, he hates, he loves.

6. Orson Pratt edited in 1853 a journal called *The Seer*, from which we take most of the following quotations.

> QUESTION 44. Can he live in several places at the same time?—No.

This material God inhabits the Planet *Colob*; he is also materially the Father of the creatures he has *begotten*, and the prophet says in his last sermon: 'God did not have the power to create the spirit of man. This idea would diminish man in my eyes; but I know better than that.' What he knew, or claimed to know, is this: initially the Mormon God was a God who 'evolved'; his origin was 'the fusion of two particles of elementary matter,' and, by a progressive development, he attained human form:

> God, *it goes without saying,* commenced by being a man, and, by a path of continual progression, he has become what he is, and he can continue to progress in the same manner eternally and indefinitely. Likewise, man can also grow in knowledge and in power as long as it pleases him. If man is thus endowed with eternal progression, there will certainly come a time when he will know as much as God now knows.

Joseph Smith says again:

> The weakest child of God who now exists on the earth, will in his time have greater domination, subjects, power, and glory than Jesus Christ or his Father have today, whereas the power and elevation of the latter will grow in the same proportion.

And Parly Pratt, brother of Orson, also developed this idea:

> What will man do when this world is overpopulated? He will make *other worlds* and fly off like a swarm of bees. And when a farmer will have too many children for his portion of earth, he will say to them: My sons, matter is infinite; create a world and populate it.

In addition, the representations of the future life are as crude as possible, and consist of details as ludicrous as the descriptions of *Summerland* by Anglo-Saxon spiritualists: 'Suppose,' says the same Parly Pratt,

> that of the population of our earth, one person in a hundred partakes of a happy resurrection; what portion could each of the Saints have? We reply: each of them could well have one hundred and fifty acres of land, which would be fully sufficient to gather manna, erect splendid dwellings, and also to cultivate flowers and all things liked by the farmer and botanist.

Another 'Apostle', Spencer, chancellor of the University of Deseret and author of the *Patriarchal Order*, also says:

> The future residence of the Saints is not something figurative; just as in this world, they will also need houses for themselves and their families. Literally, those who have been deprived of their goods, houses, land, wife, or children, will receive a hundred times more.... Abraham and Sarah will continue to multiply not only in this world, but in all the worlds to come.... The resurrection will restore your own wife, whom you will keep for eternity, and you will raise children of your own flesh.

Some spiritualists, it is true, do not even wait for the resurrection to speak to us of 'celestial marriages' and 'astral children'! But this is not all. From the idea of a God 'in the making'—an idea not exclusively theirs, as witnessed in more than one instance of modern thought—the Mormons soon passed to that of a plurality of gods forming an indefinite hierarchy. In fact, it was revealed to Smith 'that our actual Bible was no more than a truncated and perverted text that he had the mission to restore to its original purity,' and that the first verse of Genesis should be interpreted thus: 'The Godhead engenders other gods together with the heaven and the earth.' Furthermore, 'each of these gods is the special god of the spirits of all flesh which live in the world he has formed.' Finally, something more extraordinary still, a revelation from Brigham Young in 1853 informs us that the God of our planet is Adam, who is himself only another form of the archangel Michael:

> When our father Adam arrived in Eden, he took with him Eve, *one of his wives*. He helped with the organization of this world. He is Michael, the Ancient of Days. He is our father and our God, *the only God* with whom we have anything to do.

In these fantastic stories some things remind us of certain rabbinical speculations, whereas in other respects we cannot help but think of the 'pluralism' of William James. Are not the Mormons among the first to have formulated the conception, so dear to the pragmatists, of a limited God, 'the invisible king' of Wells?

The cosmology of the Mormons, as far as one can judge from the rather vague and confused expressions, is a kind of atomist monism in which consciousness or intelligence is regarded as inherent to matter. The only thing that has existed for all eternity is

> an indefinite quantity of moving and *intelligent* matter, of which each particle that now exists has existed through all the depths of eternity in a state of free locomotion. Each individual of the animal or vegetable kingdom has a living and intelligent spirit. People are only tabernacles wherein resides the eternal truth of God. When we say that there is only one God and that He is eternal, we do not designate any being in particular, but this supreme Truth which inhabits a great variety of substances.

The conception of an impersonal God which appears here seems to be in absolute contradiction with the anthropomorphic and evolutionist conception noted earlier. But no doubt it is necessary to make a distinction and to admit that the corporal God who lives on the planet *Colob* is only the chief of this hierarchy of 'particular' beings that the Mormons also call gods. We must add as well that Mormonism, the leaders of which pass through a series of 'initiations', really has an exoterism and an esoterism. But to continue: 'Each man is an aggregate of so many intelligent individuals, which he incorporates into his formation of particles of matter.' Here we find something which simultaneously recalls Leibnitzian monadism understood moreover in its most outer meaning, and the theory of 'poly-psychism' held by certain 'neo-spiritualists'. Finally, again in the same order of ideas, the president Brigham Young, in one of his sermons, proclaimed that 'the recompense of the virtuous will be an eternal progression, and the punishment of the wicked a return of their substance to the primitive elements of all things.' In several schools of occultism, those who are unable to gain immortality are similarly threatened with 'final dissolution'; and there are also some

Protestant sects, the Adventists among others, who allow for man only a 'conditional immortality'.

We think we have said enough to show the worth of the Mormon doctrines, and also to make it clear that, in spite of their singularity, their appearance does not constitute an isolated phenomenon; in short, they represent in many of their particulars, tendencies that have found multiple expressions in the contemporary world, and of which the actual development even seems a rather worrisome symptom of a mental disequilibrium that risks becoming widespread if care is not taken. In this respect, the Americans have given Europe some truly deplorable gifts.

6

GNOSIS AND THE SPIRITIST SCHOOLS

In its widest and highest meaning gnosis is knowledge; therefore true gnosticism cannot be a particular school or system but must above all be the search for integral truth. Nonetheless, it must not be thought that gnosticism must accept every doctrine whatsoever under the pretext that all contain a particle of truth, for synthesis is never reached by an amalgamation of disparate elements, as is too readily believed by minds habituated to the analytical methods of modern Western science.

Today there is much talk of unity among the different schools called spiritist, but all the efforts undertaken up to this point have remained fruitless. We believe that this will always be the case, for it is impossible to bring together doctrines so dissimilar as are those listed under the name of spiritism; such elements can never make a stable edifice. The mistake of most of these so-called spiritist doctrines is that in reality they are only materialism transposed onto another plane, and that they aim to apply to the domain of the Spirit methods used by ordinary science to study the hylic world. These experimental methods can never make known anything but mere phenomena, on which basis it is impossible to build any metaphysical theory whatsoever, for a universal principle cannot be inferred from particular facts. Moreover, the attempt to acquire a knowledge of the spiritual world by material means is obviously absurd; it is only in ourselves that we can find the principles of this knowledge, and never in outward objects.

Certain experimental investigations indeed have a relative value in their proper domain, but outside this same domain any such value is lost. This is why, for us, the investigation of so-called psychic forces, for example, can have neither more nor less interest than the investigation of any other natural force, and we have no more reason to show solidarity with the scholar who pursues this investigation than with the physicist or chemist who studies forces of other kinds. We speak of course only of the scientific investigation of so-called psychic forces and not of the practices of those who, starting from a preconception, wish to see in them the manifestation of the dead. These practices do not hold even the relative interest of an experimental science, and they possess the danger that the manipulation of any force by the ignorant always presents.

It is therefore impossible for those who seek to acquire spiritual knowledge to join with the experimenters, psychists or others, and this is not at all due to contempt for these latter, but simply because these latter do not work on the same level as themselves. It is no less impossible for them to accept doctrines with metaphysical claims that rely on an experiment base; these doctrines cannot seriously be granted any value at all and always lead to absurd consequences.

Gnosis must therefore avoid all these doctrines and base itself only on the orthodox Tradition contained in the sacred books of all peoples, a Tradition that in reality is everywhere the same despite the different forms it clothes itself with in order to adapt to every race and age. But here again great care must be taken to distinguish this true Tradition from all the erroneous interpretations and all the fantastic commentaries that have been bestowed on it in our day by a throng of more or less occultist schools, which unfortunately too often wish to speak about things of which they are ignorant. It is easy to attribute a doctrine to imaginary persons in order to lend it more authority and to claim a relation with lost initiatic centers in the furthest reaches of Tibet or on the most inaccessible summits of the Himalayas; but those who know the real initiatic centers know what to think of these pretensions.

This is enough to show that a union of so-called spiritist schools is impossible and that, moreover, even if it were possible, it would produce no worthwhile result and would consequently be far from as desirable as is thought by those who are well intentioned but insufficiently informed of what these different schools really are. In reality, the only possible union is that of all orthodox initiatic centers that have preserved the true Tradition in its original purity; but this union is not merely possible, it exists now as it has existed in all times. When the moment comes, the mysterious Thebah which contains all principles will open and show the immutable edifice of the universal Synthesis to those capable of contemplating the Light without being blinded.

From the first appearance of the journal *La Gnose* we have very clearly repudiated any solidarity with the different spiritist schools, whether occultist, Theosophist, spiritist, or any other more or less similar group, for we thought it particularly important to leave no room for doubt on this score in the minds of our readers. None of these opinions, which can be combined under the common denomination 'neo-spiritualist',[1] have any more connection with metaphysics, which alone interests us, than do the different scientific or philosophical schools of the modern West; and in addition, by virtue of their unjustified and unreasonable claims, they possess the serious drawback of being able to create among the insufficiently informed extremely regrettable confusions leading to nothing less than a reflection on others, we among them, of the discredit on the part of all who are serious that ought by right to be attached to them alone.

This is why we consider that we owe no particular circumspection to the theories in question, all the more so in that, if we did so, we are certain that their more or less authorized representatives, far from doing the same for us, would in no way be grateful to us, and would show us no less hostility; it would thus be pure weakness on our part that would do us no good, quite the contrary, and those who know our true thoughts on the subject would always reproach us for it. Thus we do not hesitate to declare that we consider all these neo-spiritist theories to be no less false in their very principle

1. One must be careful to distinguish this neo-spiritism from the spiritism that is called classical or eclectic, a doctrine doubtless of very little interest and of no value from the metaphysical point of view, but which at least offers itself as no more than a philosophical system like any other; being wholly superficial, it owes its success to this very lack of depth, which makes it especially convenient for university instruction.

and harmful to the public mentality than is, in our eyes, the modernist tendency under whatever form and in whatever domain it manifests itself.[2]

Indeed, if there is at least one point on which the Catholic church as presently oriented has all our sympathies, it is its fight against modernism.[3] The church appears to be much less preoccupied with neo-spiritism which, it is true, has perhaps not spread as far and as rapidly, and moreover is something outside of it and on another terrain, so that it can hardly do more than to point out the dangers to those of the faithful who might risk being seduced by doctrines of this kind. But if someone were to place himself outside of all confessional preoccupations, thus in a much more extended field of action, and could find a practical means of halting the spread of so many ravings and insanities presented more or less cleverly according to whether this is done by men of bad faith or mere imbeciles (and that in either case have already contributed to irremediably confusing such a large number of individuals), we think that he would thus accomplish a true work of mental health and would render an outstanding service to a considerable portion of present-day Western humanity.[4]

This cannot be our role, for on principle we forego all polemics and remain apart from all outward action and all partisan strife. Nonetheless, without leaving the strictly intellectual domain, we may as occasion arises point out the absurdities of certain doctrines or beliefs and sometimes emphasize certain statements made by the spiritists themselves in order to show how these can be used against their own doctrinal affirmations, for logic is not always their strong

2. For more on this see 'Masonic Orthodoxy' in *Studies in Freemasonry and the Compagnonnage*.

3. A fight that now, nearly nine decades after these lines were written (by the then twenty-three year old Guénon), it appears to have lost, at least as far as Vatican II and the 'official' church are concerned, Vatican II having been the great victory, at least in appearance, of modernism over the Catholic church. ED.

4. In this age rife with associations of every kind and leagues against every plague, real or imagined, one might perhaps suggest an 'Anti-occultist League' that would appeal simply to all people of common sense without any distinction of party or opinion.

point and incoherence is a widespread defect with them, visible to all who do not let themselves be taken in by pompous words and bombastic phrases which very often only hide an emptiness of thought. It is with this end in mind that we write the present chapter, reserving the right to take up the question again whenever we judge it opportune. We hope that our remarks, made in the course of reading and research that drew our attention incidentally to the incriminated theories, might, if there is still time, open the eyes of those of good faith who have gone astray among the neo-spiritualists and of whom at least some may be worthy of a better fate.

We have already made it known on many occasions that we absolutely reject the fundamental hypotheses of spiritism, namely reincarnation,[5] the possibility of communicating with the dead by material means, and the claim to demonstrate human immortality experimentally.[6] Moreover, these theories are not unique to the spiritists, the belief in reincarnation in particular being shared, by the majority of them, with the Theosophists and many occultists of different kinds. We can accept nothing from these doctrines because they are formally contrary to the most elementary principles of metaphysics; in addition, and for the same reason, they are clearly anti-traditional, and besides they were invented only during the nineteenth century, although their partisans try by every method of twisting and distorting texts to have us believe that they go back to remotest antiquity. To this end they use the most extraordinary and unexpected arguments; thus in a review that we will have the charity not to name, we recently saw the Catholic dogma of the 'resurrection of the body' interpreted in a reincarnationist sense; and it was a priest, no doubt strongly suspected of heterodoxy, who dared to make such assertions! It is true that reincarnation has never been

5. See in particular 'The Demiurge', pt. 1, chap. 1 above, and also *The Symbolism of the Cross* and *The Spiritist Fallacy.*

6. See 'Regarding the Great Architect of the Universe', in *Studies on Freemasonry and the Compagnonnage.*

explicitly condemned by the Catholic church, and some occultists do not fail to note this with obvious satisfaction at every opportunity. But they do not seem to suspect that, if this is so, it is merely because it was not even possible to conceive that a day might come when such folly could be imagined. As to the 'resurrection of the body', this is really only a defective way of speaking of 'the resurrection of the dead', which esoterically can correspond to the inclusion, in the being that has realized Universal Man, of all the states that were considered as having passed away with respect to its present state but that are eternally present in the 'permanent actuality of the extra-temporal being.'[7]

In another article in the same journal we came across an unintended and even unconscious admission amusing enough to merit a note in passing. A spiritist declares that 'truth lies in the exact relationship between the contingent and the absolute'; now, this relationship, which is that between the finite and the infinite, can rigorously be equal only to zero; draw the conclusion yourself and see if after this there remains anything of that claimed 'spiritist truth' that they offer as future 'experimental evidence'! Poor 'human child' [*sic*],[8] poor 'psycho-intellectual', that is to be 'nourished' with such a truth(?) and who is to be made to believe that he is 'made to know, love, and serve it' in a faithful imitation of what the Catholic catechism teaches in regard to its anthropomorphic God. Since in the intention of its promoters this 'spiritist teaching' seems above all to have a sentimental and moral goal, we wonder if it is worth the trouble to substitute for these old religions—which despite all their defects at least have an incontestable validity from this relative point of view—such bizarre ideas which will never replace them to advantage in any respect and which especially will be entirely unable to fulfill the social role that they claim as their own.

7. Of course this esoteric interpretation has nothing in common with the actual Catholic doctrine which is purely exoteric. On this subject see *The Symbolism of the Cross*.

8. The author takes care to warn us that 'this is not a pleonasm'; but then we have to ask what it might be.

But let us return to the question of reincarnation. This is not the place to demonstrate its metaphysical impossibility, that is to say its absurdity; we have already provided all the elements of this demonstration[9] and will complete it in further studies. For the moment we must limit ourselves to what its partisans themselves say, so that we may discover what, according their understanding, might be the basis for this belief. The spiritists want above all to demonstrate reincarnation 'experimentally'(?) by facts, and certain occultists follow them in these attempts which naturally have not yet yielded any convincing results, any more than has the 'scientific demonstration of immortality'. On the other hand, most Theosophists seem to see in the reincarnationist theory only a sort of dogma or article of faith that must be accepted for sentimental reasons, but for which it is impossible to give any rational or perceptible proof.

We beg our readers to excuse us if in what follows we are unable to give every reference precisely, for there are people whom the truth would perhaps offend. But in order to explain the reasoning by which some occultists try to prove reincarnation we must first advise the reader that those to whom we allude are supporters of the geocentric theory: they see the earth as the center of the universe, either materially in terms of physical astronomy itself, like Auguste Strindberg and others,[10] or, if they do not go this far, at least by the privilege they accord the nature of its inhabitants. For them the earth is in fact the only world where there can be human beings, because the conditions of life on other planets or in other solar systems are too different from those on Earth for a man to adapt to them; from this it follows that by 'man' they mean exclusively a corporeal individual endowed with five physical senses, the corresponding faculties (without forgetting spoken language... and even written), and all the organs necessary for the different functions of

9. See *The Symbolism of the Cross* and *The Spiritist Error.*

10. There are some who go so far as to deny the real existence of the stars and to regard them as mere reflections, virtual images or exhalations of the Earth, according to the opinion attributed, doubtless falsely, to certain ancient philosophers such as Anaximander and Anaximenes (see the translation of the *Philosophumena* pages 12 and 13); we shall speak later of the astronomical ideas peculiar to some occultists.

terrestrial human life. They do not conceive that man exists in other forms of life,[11] or with all the more reason, that he can exist in immaterial mode, informal, extra-temporal, extra-spatial, and above all beyond and above life.[12] It follows that humans can only be reincarnated on earth since there is no other place in the universe where they can live. Let us note, moreover, that this is contrary to several other ideas according to which man is 'incarnated' on various planets, as Louis Figuier holds,[13] or in different worlds, either simultaneously, as Blanqui imagines,[14] or successively, as Nietzsche's theory of the 'eternal return' tends to imply.[15] Some people have even gone so far as to claim that the human individual can have several 'material bodies'[16] [*sic*] living at the same time on different planets of the physical world.[17]

We must say further that the occultists we mentioned add, as usual accompaniment to the geocentric doctrine, a belief in the literal and popular interpretation of the Scriptures, and lose no occasion to publicly mock the triple and sevenfold meanings of the esoterists and Kabbalists.[18] Thus, according to their theory, which

11. Moreover, we can note in passing that all writers, astronomers or otherwise, who have put forth hypotheses about the inhabitants of other planets have always, perhaps unconsciously, imagined them in the more or less modified image of terrestrial human beings (see in particular C. Flammarion, *La Pluralité des Mondes habités* and *Les Mondes imaginaries at les Mondes réels*).

12. The existence of individual beings in the physical world is subject to five conditions: space, time, matter, form, and life, which can be considered as corresponding to the five bodily senses as well as the five elements; we shall treat this very important question with all the developments it implies in the course of other studies.

13. *Le Lendemain de la Mort ou la Vie future selon la Science*; see 'Regarding the Great Architect of the Universe' in *Studies on Freemasonry and the Compagnonnage*.

14. *L'Eternité des Astres*.

15. See *The Symbolism of the Cross*.

16. Here is another occasion to wonder if 'this is not a pleonasm'.

17. We have even heard the following assertion: 'If you happen to dream that you have been killed, it is in most cases because you have been on another planet'!

18. This does not prevent them from sometimes wanting to remake the Kabbalah in their own fashion; thus we have seen some who count as many as 72 Sephiroth; and it is they who dare accuse others of 'fantasizing'!

conforms to an exoteric translation of the Bible, in the beginning man, 'issuing from the hands of the Creator' (we think that no one can deny that this is anthropomorphism), was placed on Earth to 'cultivate his own garden', that is, according to them, to 'evolve physical matter,' which they suppose to have been more subtle then than today. By 'man' must be understood the entire human collectivity, the totality of the human species, so that 'all men' without any exception and in an unknown but certainly very large multitude were initially incarnated on Earth at the same time.[19] In these conditions there obviously could be no birth since there was no man who was not incarnated, and things remained this way as long as man did not die, that is, until the 'fall' understood in its exoteric sense as a historical fact,[20] but which is nevertheless regarded as 'being able to represent a whole series of events that must have unfolded over the course of several centuries.' This somewhat broadens ordinary biblical chronology, which finds it easy to place the whole history not only of the Earth but of the World, from the creation to our days, into a total duration of something less than six thousand years (some, however, go to nearly ten thousand).[21] After the 'fall' physical matter became more gross, its properties were modified, it became subject to corruption, and men, imprisoned in this matter, began to die, to 'disincarnate'; thereupon they also became subject to birth, for these 'disincarnated' men who remain 'in space'(?) in the 'invisible atmosphere' of the Earth, would then 'reincarnate', that is, once again take on earthly physical life in a new human body. Thus it is always the same human beings (it must not be forgotten that this means the restricted corporeal individuality)

19. This is not the opinion of certain other schools of occultism, which speak of 'the differences in age of human spirits' with respect to terrestrial existence and even of methods to determine them. There are also those who try to determine the number of successive incarnations.

20. On the esoteric and metaphysical interpretation of the 'original Fall' of man, see above, pt.1, chap. 1, 'The Demiurge'.

21. However, we shall not contradict the opinion that assigns to the world a duration of ten thousand years if this number is no longer taken in its literal sense but as designating numerical indefinity. (See above, pt.2, chap. 2, 'On Mathematical Notation'.)

that must be periodically reborn from the beginning of terrestrial humanity to its end.[22]

As can be seen, this reasoning is very simple and perfectly logical, but only on condition of first admitting the starting-point, that is, the impossibility of the human being existing in modalities other than the terrestrial corporeal form, which, let us repeat, can in no way be reconciled with the most elementary notions of metaphysics; and this seems to be the most solid argument that can be offered to support the hypothesis of reincarnation!

Indeed, we cannot for an instant take seriously the moral and sentimental arguments for this hypothesis, which are based on an averred injustice in the inequality of human conditions. This notion arises solely from always considering particular facts in isolation from the whole of which they form a part, while if they are again situated in this whole there can obviously be no injustice, or, to use a term that is both more exact and broader in meaning, there is no disequilibrium,[23] because these facts, like all the rest, are elements of the total harmony. We have sufficiently explained our position on

22. This implies that earthly humanity has an end, for there are schools which maintain that the goal is to regain 'physical' or 'bodily' immortality, and that each human individual will reincarnate upon Earth until he has finally attained this result. — On the other hand, according to the Theosophists, the series of each individual's incarnations in this world is limited to the duration of a single earthly human 'race', after which all men making up this 'race' will pass on to the 'sphere' determined by the 'round' they belong to. The Theosophists also maintain that as a general rule (but with exceptions) two consecutive incarnations are separated by a fixed interval of time of 15 thousand years, while according to the spiritists one can sometimes reincarnate almost immediately after death, if not while still alive(!) in certain cases which, happily, are said to be very rare. — Another question that provokes numerous and interminable controversies is to know if the same individual must always and necessarily 'reincarnate' in the same sex or whether the contrary hypothesis is possible; we may have occasion to return to this point.

23. See *L'Archéomètre*, 2nd year, no.1, p15, n3. — In the social order what is called justice can only lie in compensating injustices by other injustices, to use a Far-Eastern formula (a conception that does not suffer the introduction of mystico-moral ideas such as merit and demerit, reward and punishment, etc., any more than it does the Western idea of moral and social progress). The sum of all these injustices, which together are in harmony and equilibrium, is the greatest justice from the viewpoint of the human individual.

this question elsewhere and we have shown that evil has no reality whatsoever, that what is so called is only a relativity considered analytically, and that beyond the special point of view of the human mentality imperfection is necessarily illusory, for it cannot exist except as an element of the Perfect which can obviously contain nothing imperfect. [24]

It is easy to understand that the diversity of human conditions arises from nothing else than the differences in nature existing among individuals themselves, that it is inherent in the individual nature of earthly human beings, and that it is no more unjust or less necessary (being of the same order, although of a different species) than the variety of plant or animal species, against which no one has dreamed of protesting in the name of justice, which would be perfectly ridiculous.[25] The special conditions belonging to each individual work toward the perfection of the total being of which this individual is a modality or particular state, and in the totality of the being everything is joined and given equilibrium by the harmonious linking of cause and effect.[26] But once it is a matter of causality, no one who possesses the least idea of metaphysics can understand this to mean anything even remotely resembling the mystico-religious idea of reward and punishment,[27] which, after having been applied to an extra-terrestrial 'future life' is applied by the neo-spiritualists to supposed 'successive lives' on Earth, or at least in the physical world.[28]

24. See 'The Demiurge', pt. 1, chap 1 above.

25. On the question of the diversity of human conditions considered as the basis of castes, see *L'Archéomètre*, 2nd year, no.1 pp8 ff.

26. This supposes the coexistence of all the elements considered outside of time as well as outside of every other contingent condition belonging to any specialized mode of existence. Let us note once more that this coexistence obviously leaves no room for the idea of progress.

27. To this idea of religious sanctions belongs the wholly Western theory of sacrifice and expiation, the inanity of which we shall demonstrate.

28. What the Theosophists most incorrectly call *Karma* is nothing other than the law of causality, which, moreover, they understand very poorly and apply even less well. We say that they understand it badly, that is to say incompletely, for they restrict it to the individual domain instead of extending it to the indefinite multitude of states of the being. In reality, the Sanskrit word *Karma*, which derives from

The spiritists, especially, have exploited this wholly anthropomorphic idea and have drawn from it conclusions that often reach the extreme of absurdity. Such is the well known example of the victim who pursues vengeance against his murderer into another existence; the victim then becomes murderer in his turn and the murderer, now a victim, must avenge himself in a new existence, and so on indefinitely. Another example of the same sort is the coachman who runs over a pedestrian; as punishment, the coachman, who has become a pedestrian in the next life, will be run over by the pedestrian who has become a coachman; but logically this coachman must then suffer the same punishment, so that these two unhappy individuals will be obliged to run each other over alternately until the end of time, for there is obviously no reason why this should come to an end.

But to be impartial we must add that on this point certain occultists concede nothing to the spiritists, for we have heard one occultist give the following account as an example of the frightful consequences that can follow upon actions generally considered indifferent.[29] A student amuses himself by breaking a pen, then throws it away; the molecules of metal will retain the memory of the mischief committed against them by the child throughout all the transformations they will undergo; finally, after several centuries, these molecules will enter into the parts of some machine and, one day, there will be an accident and a worker will be killed, crushed by this machine; it will turn out that the worker is the student described earlier, who has been reincarnated to suffer the punishment for his

the verbal root *kri*, 'to make' (identical to the Latin *creare*), simply means 'action' and nothing else. The Westerners who use it thus have turned it from its true meaning, of which they are ignorant, and they have done the same for a great number of other Eastern terms.

29. It goes without saying that the purely individual (and imaginary) consequences in question here have no connection with the metaphysical theory, of which we shall speak elsewhere, that the most elementary gesture can have unlimited consequences in the Universal by reverberating and amplifying throughout the indefinite series of states of the being, both horizontally and vertically (see *The Symbolism of the Cross*).

earlier act.[30] It would surely be difficult to imagine anything more extravagant than such fantastic tales, which suffice to give an accurate picture of the mentality of those who invent them and especially of those who believe them.

An idea closely linked to reincarnation, which also has many partisans among neo-spiritualists, is that in the course of its evolution each being must pass successively through all forms of life, terrestrial and otherwise.[31] To this there is only one word in response: such a theory is an impossibility for the simple reason that there exist an indefinity of living forms through which a being could never pass since these forms are occupied by other beings. It is therefore absurd to claim that a being must traverse all possibilities considered individually in order to reach the term of its evolution because this affirmation encloses an impossibility; and here we can see a particular case of that entirely false idea, so widespread in the West, that a synthesis can only be accomplished by analysis, whereas on the contrary it is impossible to achieve it in this fashion.[32] Even if a being should have traversed an indefinity of possibilities, this entire evolution could never be anything but rigorously zero with respect to Perfection, for the indefinite proceeds from the finite; and since indefinity is produced by the finite (as the generation of numbers clearly shows) and is thus contained in it in potency, in the final analysis it is only the development of the potentialities of the finite and in consequence obviously cannot have any connection with the Infinite, which amounts to saying that, considered from the standpoint of the Infinite (or from Perfection, which is identical with the Infinite), it can be only zero.[33] The analytic conception of evolution

30. There are occultists who go so far as to claim that congenital infirmities are the result of accidents that occurred in 'earlier existences'.

31. We speak only of 'forms of life' because it must be clearly understood that those who hold such an opinion can conceive nothing outside of life (and of life in a form) so that for them this expression encloses all possibilities, while for us it represents on the contrary only a very special possibility of manifestation.

32. See 'The Demiurge', pt. 1, chap. 1 above.

33. What is generally true of the indefinite considered in connection (or rather in its absence of connection) with the Infinite remains true for each particular aspect of the indefinite or, if you will, for the particular indefinite corresponding to

is thus reduced to adding zero to itself indefinitely by an indefinite number of successive and distinct additions, the final result of which will always be zero. This sterile succession of analytical operations can be transcended only by integration, and this is accomplished at one stroke by a transcendent and immediate synthesis that logically has no preceding analysis.[34]

Moreover, since, as we have explained on various occasions, the entire physical world, with the deployment of all the possibilities it contains, is only the domain of manifestation of a single state of the individual being, this same state of the being contains in itself *a fortiori* the potentialities for all the modalities of terrestrial life, which represents only a very restricted portion of the physical world. Thus, if the complete development of the actual individuality, which extends indefinitely beyond the corporeal modality, includes all the potentialities whose manifestation constitutes the sum of the physical world, it includes in particular all those corresponding to the different modalities of terrestrial life. This therefore renders useless the supposition of a multiplicity of existences through which the being must progressively raise itself from the lowest modality of life, the mineral, to the human modality considered as the highest, passing successively through plant and animal modalities, with all the multiplicity of degrees contained in each of these kingdoms. In his integral extension the individual simultaneously contains the possibilities that correspond to all these degrees; this simultaneity is not expressed in temporal succession except in the development of his corporeal modality, during which, as embryology shows, he passes through all the corresponding stages from the unicellular form of the most elementary organized beings, and, going back still further, even from the crystal (which presents more than one analogy with

the development of each possibility considered in isolation. It is therefore true of immortality (indefinite extension of the possibility of life) which in consequence can be nothing but zero with regard to Eternity. On this point we shall have the opportunity to explain ourselves more fully elsewhere (see also 'Regarding the Great Architect of the Universe' in *Studies in Freemasonry and the Compagnonnage*).

34. For more details on the mathematical representation of the totalization of the being by a double integration that realizes the universal volume, see our study *The Symbolism of the Cross.*

these rudimentary beings),[35] to the terrestrial human form. But for us these considerations are in no way a proof of the 'transformist' theory, for we regard the so-called law that 'ontogeny recapitulates phylogeny' as a pure hypothesis; for if the development of the individual, or ontogeny, can be proved by direct observation, no one would dare to claim that the same goes for the development of the species, or phylogeny.[36] Moreover, even in the restricted sense just noted, the point of view of succession loses almost all its interest by the simple observation that the seed, before any development, already contains in potency the complete being; and this point of view must always remain subordinate to that of simultaneity, to which the metaphysical theory of the multiple states of the being necessarily leads us.

Thus, leaving to one side the essentially relative question of the embryonic development of the body (which we see only as indicating an analogy with the integral individuality), there can be no question of anything but a purely logical (and not temporal) succession, that is to say a hierarchization of these modalities or possibilities in the extension of the individual state of the being in which they are not realized corporeally, and this because of the simultaneous existence in the individual of an indefinitude of vital modalities, or, what amounts to the same thing, the corresponding possibilities. In this connection, and to show that these ideas are not peculiar to us, we thought it would be interesting to reproduce certain extracts from a chapter devoted to this question in the instruction manuals of one of the rare serious initiatic Fraternities that still exist today in the West:[37]

35. Particularly in regard to growth; likewise for reproduction by bipartition or twinning; on the question of the life of crystals, see in particular the noteworthy works of J.C. Bose of Calcutta, which have in turn inspired works by various European thinkers.

36. We have already explained why the purely scientific question of 'transformism' has no interest for metaphysics (see 'Scientific Conceptions and Masonic Ideal' in *Studies in Freemasonry and the Compagnonnage*).

37. We will not pause to point out the absurd calumnies and inept tales that ill-informed or ill-intentioned people have wantonly spread about this Fraternity, which is designated by the initials 'H B of L.' [Regarding the Hermetic Brotherhood

In the descent of life into outward conditions, the monad had to travel through each of the states of the spiritual world, then the kingdoms of the astral empire,[38] in order to appear at last on the outward plane, the lowest possible, that is to say the mineral plane. From that point we see it successively penetrate the waves of mineral, plant, and animal life of the planet. In virtue of the higher and most inward laws of its particular cycle, its divine attributes always seek to unfold their imprisoned potentialities. As soon as one form is provided and its capacities are exhausted[39] another, new form of a higher degree is requisitioned; thus each in its turn becomes more and more complex in structure, more and more diverse in function. Thus we see the living monad begin with the mineral in the *outward* world, then the great *spiral* of its evolutionary existence moves slowly forward, imperceptibly but nevertheless always progressing.[40] There is no form too simple nor organism too complex for the faculty of adaptation (a marvelous and inconceivable power) possessed by the human soul. And through the entire cycle of Necessity the character of its genius, the degree of its spiritual emanation, and the states to which it belonged at the beginning are strictly preserved with a mathematical exactitude.[41]

During the course of its involution the monad is not really incarnated in any form whatever. The course of its descent through the various kingdoms comes about by a gradual polarization of its divine powers due to its contact with the conditions of gradual externalization of the descending and subjective arc of the spiral cycle.

of Luxor, see *The Spiritist Fallacy*, pt.1, chap. 2, and *Theosophy: History of a Pseudo-Religion*, chaps. 2 and 3]; but we believed that it is nonetheless necessary to advise that it is foreign to all occultist movements, although some of these have judged it good to appropriate some of its teachings, distorting them completely to adapt them to their own ideas.

38. That is, the various states of subtle manifestation divided according to their correspondence with the elements.

39. That is to say that it has completely developed the entire series of modifications of which it is capable.

40. This is from the *outward* point of view, of course.

41. This indeed implies the *coexistence* of all the vital modalities.

This is an absolute truth expressed by the adept author of *Ghost Land* when he says that, *as an impersonal being*, man lives in an indefinite number of worlds before arriving in this one. In all these worlds, the soul develops its rudimentary states until its cyclic progress makes it capable of attaining[42] the special state whose glorious function is to confer *consciousness* on this soul. It is only at this moment that it truly becomes a man; in every other instant of its cosmic voyage it was but an embryonic being, a passing form, an impersonal creature in which shines a part, but only a part, of the *non-individualized* human soul.
Once the great stage of *consciousness* has been reached, summit of the series of material manifestations, the soul will *never* again enter into the matrix of matter, will never again undergo *material incarnation*; henceforth *its rebirths are all in the kingdom of the spirit.* Those who maintain the strangely illogical doctrine of the multiplicity of *human* births have surely never developed in themselves the lucid state of spiritual consciousness; otherwise the theory of reincarnation, asserted and maintained today by a great number of men and women versed in 'worldly wisdom', would not be given the least credit. An *outward* education is relatively worthless as a means of obtaining *true* Knowledge.

No analogy favoring reincarnation is found in nature, while on the other hand, many are found favoring the contrary.

The acorn becomes oak, the coconut becomes palm; but let the oak produce myriads of other acorns, it will never again become an acorn itself, nor will the palm once again become coconut. The same for man: once the soul is manifested on the human plane and has thus reached consciousness of outward life, it never again passes through any of its rudimentary states.
A recent publication asserts that 'those who have led a noble life worthy of a king (be this in the body of a beggar) in their last earthly existence will come to life again as nobles, kings, or other persons of high rank'! But we know that kings and nobles

42. By the gradual extension of this development to the point where it attains a determinate zone that corresponds to the particular state here under consideration.

> in the past have been and in the present are often the worst specimens of humanity that can be conceived from the spiritual point of view. Such assertions serve only to prove that their authors only speak under the inspiration of sentimentality and that they lack Knowledge.
>
> All the alleged 're-awakening of latent memories' by which some people try to insure the recall of their past existences can be explained and even solely explained by simple laws of *affinity* and of *form*. Each race of human beings considered *in itself* is immortal; it is the same for each cycle: the first cycle never becomes the second, but the beings of the first cycle are (spiritually) the parents or *generators* of those of the second.[43] Thus each cycle includes a great family made up of the reunion of the different groups of human souls, each condition being determined by the laws of its *activity*, those of its *form*, and those of its *affinity*—a triad of laws.
>
> This is why man can be compared to the acorn and the oak: the embryonic soul, un-individualized, becomes a man just as the acorn becomes an oak, and just as the oak gives birth to an innumerable quantity of acorns, so man in his turn provides an indefinite number of souls with the means to be born in the spiritual world. There is a complete correspondence between the two, and it is for this reason that the ancient Druids paid such great honors to this tree, which was honored above all the others by the powerful Hierophants.

From this one can see how far the Druids were from admitting 'transmigration' in the ordinary and material sense of the word, and how little they dreamed of the theory—which, we repeat, is wholly modern—of reincarnation.

43. This is why the Hindu tradition gives the name of *Pitris* (fathers or ancestors) to the beings of the cycle preceding ours, which is represented with regard to ours as corresponding to the Sphere of the Moon. The *Pitris* make terrestrial humanity in their image and present humanity plays in its turn the same role toward the following cycle. This causal relation of one cycle to another necessarily presupposes the coexistence of all cycles, which are successive only from the point of view of their logical sequence; if it were otherwise, such a relation could not exist (see *Man and His Becoming according to the Vedānta*).

WE have recently read in a foreign spiritist journal an article in which the author criticizes with good reason the preposterous idea of those who announce the impending 'second coming' of Christ as necessarily being a reincarnation.[44] But where things become rather amusing is when the same author declares that if this thesis cannot be admitted, it is simply because according to him the return of Christ is even now an accomplished fact... thanks to spiritism!

'It has already happened,' says he, 'because in certain centers his communications are registered.' One must truly have a very robust faith in order to thus believe that Christ and his Apostles reveal themselves in spiritist seances and speak through the mouthpiece of mediums! If there are people for whom such a belief is necessary (and this seems to be the case with the great majority of Westerners) we do not hesitate to assert how much we still prefer the belief of the least enlightened Catholic or even the faith of the sincere materialist, for this also exists.[45]

As we have already said, we think that neo-spiritism in any form is absolutely incapable of replacing the ancient religions in their social and moral roles, and nevertheless this is certainly the goal it proposes in a more or less open way. Earlier we alluded in particular to the claims of its promoters for education; in fact we just read a speech on this subject by one of them. Whatever he may have said on the subject, we find very little stability in the 'liberal spiritualism' of those 'aviators of the spirit'(?!) who, seeing in the atmosphere 'two colossal rain clouds full to the jaws [*sic*] with contrary electricities', ask 'how to avoid the series of lightning flashes, the scales of thunder [*sic*], the cataracts of lighting, and who despite these threatening omens wish to brave the freedom of education' as others have 'braved the freedom of space'. They nonetheless admit that 'education in the schools must remain neutral', but on condition that this

44. This bizarre opinion, which for some years has found much credit among the Theosophists, is after all hardly more absurd than the opinion that St John the Baptist was a reincarnation of the prophet Elijah; we will say a few words later on about the different Gospel texts that some people have endeavored to interpret in favor of the reincarnationist theory.

45. See 'Regarding the Great Architect of the Universe' in *Studies in Freemasonry and the Compagnonnage*.

'neutrality' lead to 'spiritualist' conclusions. It seems to us that this would only be an apparent neutrality, not a real one, and whoever has the least sense of logic can hardly think otherwise. But for them, on the contrary, this is 'profound neutrality'! A systematic mentality and preconceived ideas sometimes lead to strange contradictions, and this is an example that we wished to point out.[46] As for us, who are far from aspiring to any social action, it is obvious that this question of education thus posed cannot interest us in any way. The only method that could have a real value would be 'integral instruction',[47] and unfortunately, given the present mentality, it will no doubt be a long time before the least application of this can be made in the West, particularly in France, where the Protestant mentality so dear to certain 'liberal spiritualists' reigns as the absolute master at all levels and in all branches of government.

RECENTLY the author of the speech in question (we do not wish to name him here in order not to wound his... modesty, and the circumstances do not matter) decided it was good to reproach us for having said that we have 'absolutely nothing in common with him' (no more than with the other neo-spiritualists of any sect or school), and he objected that this must lead us to 'reject comradeship, virtue, to deny God, the immortality of the soul, and Christ'—a rather disparate collection of things! Although we formally forbid ourselves any polemics in this Journal we think that it would not be useless to reproduce here our response to these objections, for a more complete enlightenment of our readers and to mark more clearly and more precisely (at the risk of repeating ourselves somewhat) certain profound differences which we cannot emphasize too much.

First of all, whatever Mr X may say..., his God is certainly not ours, for he evidently believes, as do all modern Westerners, in a

46. In this connection but in another order of ideas we can recall the attitude of certain scholars who refuse to admit facts duly proved simply because their theories cannot provide a satisfactory explanation of them.

47. See *L'instruction intégrale* by our eminent collaborator F. Ch. Barlet.

'personal' (not to say individual) and rather anthropomorphic God who has 'nothing in common' with the metaphysical Infinite.[48] We will say as much of his idea of Christ, that is to say a unique Messiah who is an 'incarnation' of the Divinity; we on the contrary recognize a plurality (and even an indefinite number) of divine 'manifestations' which are not in any way 'incarnations', for above all it is important to maintain the purity of monotheism, which cannot agree with such a theory.

As to the individualistic idea of the 'immortality of the soul', this is even simpler, and Mr X... is strangely mistaken if he believes that we hesitate to state that we reject it completely, both in the form of an extra-terrestrial 'future life', as well as in the surely much more ridiculous and all too well known theory of 'reincarnation'. Questions of 'pre-existence' and 'post-existence' obviously do not arise for anyone who envisages all things outside of time; moreover, 'immortality' can only be an indefinite extension of life, and it will never be otherwise than rigorously equivalent to *zero* in the face of Eternity,[49] which alone interests us, and which is above life as well as time and all the other limitative conditions of individual existence. We know very well that Westerners are attached above all to their 'I'; but what value can a purely sentimental tendency like this have? Too bad for those who prefer illusory consolations to the Truth!

Finally, 'fraternity' and 'virtue' are manifestly nothing other than mere moral concepts; and morality, which is wholly relative and concerns only the very particular and restricted domain of social action,[50] has absolutely nothing to do with Gnosis, which is *exclusively metaphysical.* And we do not think we are 'risking' too much, as Mr X says, in asserting that he is

48. Moreover the word *God* [*Dieu*] itself is so linked to the anthropomorphic conception [of the Divine] and has become so incapable of corresponding to anything else, that we prefer to avoid using it as much as possible, be this only to better mark the abyss that separates metaphysics from the religions.

49. See above, p158, n33.

50. On this question of morality see 'Scientific Conceptions and Masonic Ideal', cited above.

> *entirely* ignorant of metaphysics; this being said, moreover, without reproaching him in the least, for it is incontestably allowable to be ignorant of what one has never had the occasion to study; no one is held to the impossible!

We said earlier, but without dwelling on it, that there are people, spiritists and others, who strive to prove the reincarnationist thesis 'experimentally'.[51] Such an attempt must appear so improbable to any person with the least amount of common sense that one is tempted *a priori* to suppose it to be merely a bad joke; but it seems that it is not. Indeed, an experimenter of serious repute who has acquired a certain scientific esteem for his work on 'psychism'[52] but who, unfortunately for him, seems little by little to have been converted almost entirely to the spiritist theories (it frequently happens that scholars are not exempt from a certain... naiveté),[53] has quite recently published a work containing a description of his researches into so called 'successive lives' by means of the phenomena of 'memory regression' which he believes he has seen in certain subjects of hypnosis or magnetism.[54]

51. See *The Spiritist Fallacy*, chapter on reincarnation [pt. 2, chap. 6].

52. Lacking a less imperfect term we retain 'psychism', as vague and imprecise as it is, to designate all the studies of which the object is itself hardly better defined. Someone (Dr Richet we believe) had the unfortunate idea of substituting the word 'metapsychics', which has the immense drawback of making one think of something more or less analogous or parallel to metaphysics (and in this case we do not see clearly what that could be if not metaphysics itself under another name), while on the contrary this is an experimental science with methods modeled as exactly as possible on those of the physical sciences.

53. The case we allude to is not isolated and similar ones exist of which many are well known. Elsewhere we cited the cases of Crookes, Lobroso, Dr Richet, and Camille Flammarion ('Regarding the Great Architect of the Universe') and we could have added that of William James and many others besides. All of this merely proves that an analytic scholar, whatever his value as such and whatever his special domain, is not, outside of this domain, necessarily much better off than the great mass of the ignorant and credulous public who furnish the major part of the spirito-occultist clientele.

54. We shall not investigate here how far it is possible to clearly distinguish hypnotism and magnetism; it could indeed be that this distinction is more verbal than real and, in any case, it has no importance to the question that now occupies us.

We say: 'which he believes he has seen', for while we do not in any way wish to doubt his good faith, we think that the facts that he interprets in this way by virtue of a preconceived hypothesis are really explained in another, much simpler way. These facts can be summed up as follows: The subject, being in a certain state, can be placed mentally in conditions where he finds himself in a past age, and to be thus 'situated' at some age or another about which he then speaks as if it were the present, whence it is concluded that in this case there is no 'remembrance' but 'memory regression'. This latter, by the way, is a contradiction in terms, for there can obviously be no question of memory where there is no remembering; but leaving this observation aside, it must first be asked if the possibility of remembrance pure and simple is truly excluded for the sole reason that the subject speaks of the past as if it were present to him again.

To this one can immediately respond that memories as such are always mentally present;[55] what marks them in our present consciousness as memories of past events is their comparison with our present perceptions (we mean present as perceptions), a comparison that only allows one to be distinguished from the other by the establishment of a relationship (temporal, that is, of succession) between outward events[56] of which they are for us the respective mental representations. If for some reason (either by the momentary suppression of every outward impression or in some other way), this comparison comes to be impossible, memory, no longer localized in time with respect to other psychological elements at present different, loses its characteristic quality of past and preserves only its quality of present. Now this is precisely what happens in the case we are considering. The state in which the subject is

55. It matters little whether these memories are actually in the field of clear and distinct consciousness, or in that of the 'subconscious' (taking this word in its most general sense), since normally they can always pass from one to the other, which shows that this is only a difference of degree and nothing more.

56. Outward with respect to the point of view of our individual consciousness, of course; this distinction between memory and perception belongs to the most elementary psychology and, on the other hand, it is independent of the question of the mode of perception of the objects regarded as outward, or rather of their sensible qualities.

placed corresponds to a modification of his present consciousness, implying an extension of the individual faculties in a certain direction to the momentary detriment of the development in another direction that these faculties possess in their normal state. If therefore the subject is prevented in such a state from being affected by present perceptions and if, further, all events after a certain determinate moment are kept from his consciousness (conditions that are perfectly attainable with the help of suggestion), they cannot be situated in the past or considered in this aspect because in the present field of consciousness there is no longer any element to which they can be related as temporally past.

In all of this it is a question of nothing more than a mental state implying a modification of the conception of time (or better, of its comprehension) with respect to the normal state; moreover, these two states are both only two different modifications of one and the same individuality.[57] Indeed, there can be no question of higher and extra-individual states in which the being is freed from the temporal condition, nor even of an extension of the individuality implying such freedom in part, since on the contrary the subject is placed in a determinate instant which essentially presupposes that his present state is conditioned by time. Besides, on the one hand states like those to which we have just alluded obviously cannot be reached by means that remain entirely within the domain of the present and restricted individuality, as every experimental process necessarily is; on the other hand, even if these states should in some way be reached, they could never be discerned by this individuality whose particular conditions of existence have no contact with those of the higher states, and because, as a particular individuality, it is necessarily incapable of assenting to, and *a fortiori* of expressing, all that is above the limits of its own possibilities.[58]

57. The same goes for the states (spontaneous or induced) corresponding to all the alterations of individual consciousness, the most important of which are usually ranged under the improper and defective name of 'split personality'.

58. Besides, all the cases we are considering involve only physical events, and even, most often, terrestrial ones (although another well known experimenter once published a detailed description of supposed 'earlier incarnations' of his subject on

As for really returning to the past, this is something which is as we have said elsewhere manifestly just as impossible for the human individual as is travel into the future;[59] and we never would have thought that Wells' 'time machine'[60] could have been considered to be anything but pure fantasy, nor that anyone would come to speak seriously about the 'reversibility of time'. Space is reversible, that is to say that after any one of its parts has been traversed in a given direction it can thereafter be traversed in the opposite direction; this is because it is a coordination of elements considered in present and permanent mode; but time, on the contrary, is a coordination of elements considered in successive and transitory mode and thus cannot be reversible, for such a supposition would be the very negation of the point of view of succession, or, in other words, it would amount precisely to the abolition of the temporal condition.[61] Nonetheless there are people who have conceived this singular—to say the least—idea of the 'reversibility of time' and who have attempted to base it on a 'theorem of mechanics'(?) which we believe interesting enough to reproduce in its entirety in order to show more clearly the origin of their fantastic hypothesis.

> The complex series of all the successive states of a system of bodies being known, and these states following and developing from each other in a determinate order from the past, which serves as cause, to the future, which has the rank of effect [*sic*], let us then

the planet Mars, without being surprised that all that happened there should be so easily described in earthly language!); there is nothing in all of this that requires the least intervention of the higher states of the being, the existence of which the 'psychists' do not of course even suspect.

59. For this and for what follows see our study on 'The Conditions of Corporeal Existence'.

60. H.G. Wells, 1866–1946, English novelist with a taste for science fiction and 'progress'. Ed.

61. This abolition of the temporal condition is indeed possible, but not in the cases we are considering here, since these cases always presuppose time; and when speaking elsewhere of the 'eternal present' we have been very careful to point out that this can have nothing to do with a return to the past or traveling into the future since it precisely abolishes the past and the future by freeing us from the viewpoint of succession, that is to say from what constitutes for our present being, the whole reality of the temporal condition.

> consider one of these successive states, and without changing anything of the composing masses or of the forces that act between these masses,[62] or of the laws of these forces nor of the present situations of these masses in space, let us replace each velocity by an equal and contrary velocity.[63] We shall call this 'reverting' all the speeds; this change itself will take the name of reversion, and we shall call its possibility reversibility of the movement of the system.

Let us pause a moment here, for it is precisely this possibility that we cannot admit even from the point of view of movement, which is necessarily effected in time; in a new series of successive states but in the opposite direction, the system under consideration will regain the positions that it had earlier occupied in space, but time will never be the same as before, and it is obviously sufficient for one condition to change in order that the new states of the system be completely unable to identify with the preceding ones. Moreover, in the reasoning that we cited, it is explicitly supposed (although in rather dubious French) that the relation of past to future is a relation of cause and effect, while on the contrary the causal relationship essentially implies simultaneity, whence the result that from this point of view the states considered to follow each other cannot develop from one another.[64] But let us continue:

> Now when the reversion of velocities in a system of bodies has been effected,[65] the complete series of future and past states for

62. 'On these masses' would have been more comprehensible.

63. A velocity contrary to another or indeed in a different direction cannot be equal to it in the rigorous sense of the word, it can only be equivalent to it in quantity; on the other hand, is it possible to consider this 'reversal' as changing nothing of the laws of the movement under consideration, given that, if these laws had continued to be followed normally, it would not have been produced?

64. *Man and His Becoming according to the Vedānta.* Consequently, if the memory of some impression can be the cause of other mental phenomena, this is as a present memory, but the past impression cannot now be the cause of anything.

65. The author of the argument had the prudence to add parenthetically 'not in reality but in pure thought'; by this he completely leaves the domain of mechanics and what he speaks of no longer has any connection with 'a system of bodies'; but it

> this reverted system must be found. Will this inquiry be any more difficult than the corresponding problem for the successive states of a non-reverted system? Neither more nor less,[66] and the solution to one of these problem will give the solution to the other by a very simple change, that in technical terms consists in changing the algebraic sign for time, writing –t instead of +t, and inversely.

This is indeed very simple in theory, but leaving aside the fact that the notation of 'negative numbers' is only a wholly artificial process meant to simplify calculations and that it does not correspond to any kind of reality, the author of this argument falls into a serious error that is shared, moreover, by almost all mathematicians, and in order to interpret the change of sign that he has just noted he immediately adds:

> That is to say that the two complete series of successive states of the same system of bodies differ only in that the future becomes past and the past becomes future.[67] The same series of successive states will be traversed in the opposite direction. The reversion of velocities simply reverses time; the original series of successive states and the reverted series have at all corresponding moments the same systemic figures with the same equal and contrary velocities [*sic*].

Unfortunately, the reversion of velocities really only reverses the spatial situations and not time; instead of being 'the same series of successive states traversed in the opposite direction' there will be a second series inversely homologous to the first with respect only to

---

is to be remembered that he himself considers the so-called 'reversion' unrealizable, contrary to the hypothesis of those who would like to apply his argument to 'memory regression'.

66. Evidently, since in both cases one examines a movement of which all the elements are given; but in order for this investigation to correspond to anything real or even possible one must not let oneself be fooled by mere changes in notation!

67. This is certainly a peculiar phantasmagoria, and it must be acknowledged that an operation as common as a mere change of algebraic sign is endowed with a most strange and truly marvelous power... in the eyes of mathematicians!

space. This will not make the past become the future, and the future will not become the past except in virtue of the normal and natural law of succession, as this occurs at every instant. It is truly too easy to show the unconscious and multiple sophisms hidden behind such arguments; yet this is all they can find to show us in justification, 'before science and philosophy', of a theory like that of so-called 'memory regressions'!

This being said, in order to complete the psychological explanations mentioned at the beginning, we must also point out that the claimed 'return to the past' (which is really only a recalling to clear and distinct consciousness of memories preserved in a latent state in the subconscious memory of the subject) is facilitated from the psychological point of view by the fact that every impression necessarily leaves a trace in the organism that has experienced it. Here we do not have to investigate the way in which this impression may be recorded in various nerve centers; this is an investigation that belongs to experimental science pure and simple, which, moreover, has already been able to 'localize' almost exactly the centers corresponding to the different modalities of the memory.[68] The action exerted on these centers, aided by the psychological factor of suggestion, allows the subject to be placed in the desired conditions to realize the experiences we discussed, at least as to their first part, that relating to events in which he has really played a role or has witnessed at a more or less remote period.[69]

68. This 'localization' is made possible especially by observing different cases of 'paramnesia' (partial alterations of the memory); and we can add that the sort of fractionating of the memory witnessed in these cases allows one to explain a great number of the so-called 'double personalities' referred to earlier.

69. As strange as this might appear at first sight, one could also speak of a correspondence, as much physiological as psychological, with events not yet realized but the virtualities of which the individual bears within himself. These virtualities are expressed by predispositions and tendencies of various kinds that are like the present seed of future events that concern the individual. Every diathesis is ultimately an organic predisposition of this kind; an individual carries within himself, from his origin (*ab ovo*, one could say) this or that illness in a latent state, but this illness might not manifest itself except in circumstances favorable to its development, for example, under the effect of some trauma or any other cause that weakens the organism. If these circumstances are not met, the illness will never develop

But of course the physiological correspondence that we just pointed out is possible only for impressions that have really affected the subject's organism; likewise from the psychological point of view the individual consciousness of some being can obviously not contain anything except elements that have some connection with the actual individuality of this being. This should suffice to show that it is useless to pursue experimental investigations beyond certain limits, that is, in the present case, before the birth of the subject, or at least before the beginning of his embryonic life; yet it is this that they claim to do on the basis of the preconceived hypothesis of reincarnation (as we said), and they think they are thus able to 'revive' the subject's 'anterior lives' while in the interval also studying 'what is taken to be the non-incarnated spirit'!

Here we are in complete fantasy. How can one speak of the 'anteriority of the living being' when it is a question of a time when this living being did not yet exist in the individualized state; and how can one wish to take him back before his origin, that is to say into conditions in which he never existed, thus conditions that for him do not correspond to any reality? This amounts to creating an artificial reality from scratch, if one may express oneself thus, that is to say a present mental reality that is not the representation of any kind of sensible reality; the suggestion given by the experimenter provides the starting-point for it, and the imagination of the subject does the rest. The same thing, minus the initial suggestion, happens in the state of ordinary dreams where the 'individual soul creates a world that comes entirely from itself and whose objects consist exclusively in mental images'[70] without it being possible to distinguish these images from perceptions originating from outside, at least as long as no comparison is established between these two kinds of psychological elements, which can only occur by a more or less clearly conscious passage from the dream state to the state of waking.[71] Thus an induced dream, a state similar in every respect to

---

in the organism, just as a psychological tendency that does not manifest itself by an outward act is no less real despite this.

70. See *Man and His Becoming according to the Vedānta.*

71. But this comparison is never possible in the case of a dream induced by suggestion since at his wakening the subject preserves no memory of it in his normal consciousness.

those in which partially or wholly imaginary perceptions are provoked in a subject by the appropriate suggestions, but with this one difference that here the experimenter is himself the dupe of his own suggestion and takes the mental creations of the subject for the 'awakening of memories'[72]—behold what the would-be 'exploration of successive lives' is reduced to, the sole 'experimental proof' that the reincarnationists have been able to furnish in favor of their theory.

That an attempt should be made to apply suggestion to 'psychotherapy', to use it to heal drunkards or maniacs or to develop the mentality of certain idiots, is an endeavor that does not fail to be most praiseworthy, and whatever the results obtained, we shall not change our opinion on the matter. But let this be the limit and let there be an end to the use of phantasmagorias like those of which we have just spoken. Nevertheless, people will still come forth to vaunt the 'clarity and evidence of spiritism' and oppose it to the 'obscurity of metaphysics', which they confuse with the most commonplace philosophy;[73] peculiar evidence, at least if it is not evidence of absurdity! But all of this does not surprise us in the least, for we know very well that the spiritists and other 'psychists' of different ilks are all like a certain person with whom we recently had dealings; they are profoundly ignorant of what metaphysics is, and we shall certainly not undertake to explain it to them. *Sarebbe lavar la testa all' asino* [Let them wash the head of a donkey],[74] as they irreverently say in Italian.

72. Moreover, the subject could also consider them to be memories, for a dream can include memories as well as present impressions, without the two kinds of element being anything more than pure mental creations. We are not of course speaking of waking memories that often mingle with a dream, because the separation of the two states of consciousness is rarely complete, at least with regard to ordinary sleep. They seem to be much more separate in induced sleep, and this is what explains the complete forgetting that follows the awakening of the subject.

73. Some even go so far as to claim they have had 'metaphysical experiences' without realizing that the juncture of these two words constitutes a pure and simple 'non-sense'.

74. A close English equivalent would be 'Let them try to make a silk purse from a sow's ear.' ED.

7

CONCERNING A MISSION TO CENTRAL ASIA

AT THE MOMENT there is much talk of the discoveries that Paul Péllliot, a former student of the French School of the Far East, appears to have made during a recent exploration of Central Asia. So many French and foreign missions have succeeded one another in this region without any appreciable results that one is permitted to be a little skeptical at first. No doubt, explorers have brought back documents that are interesting from the geographical point of view, especially photographs, as well as zoological, botanical, and mineral specimens, but nothing more. But here is what Péllliot himself relates about his expedition, first at a conference held at the Sorbonne on December 11 [1909]and then in an article that appeared in *Echo de Paris* on December 15 and 16. To learn of his archeological discoveries we can best refer to his own account.

Near the village of Tumchuk in Chinese Turkestan, he says he first found a group of ruins almost entirely buried, from which he was able to extricate some Buddhist sculptures exhibiting very clear traces of Hellenic influence. Then, at Kutchar, one of the principal oases of Chinese Turkestan, he excavated 'some artificial grottoes furnished as Buddhist sanctuaries and decorated with murals', as well as open air temples; 'in the court of one of these there one day came to light a thick pile of manuscripts all in confusion and mixed with sand and salt crystal,' in short, in rather bad shape.

> To separate the pages required much time and the attention of expert hands; thus these documents have not been deciphered. All that can be said about them at the moment is that they are written in the Hindu script called Brahmi but translated for the most part into those mysterious Central Asian languages that European philology has hardly begun to understand.

Thus Pélliot himself recognizes that the philologists, of whom he is one, have only a very imperfect knowledge of certain Asian languages; this is a point we shall return to later. For the moment, let us note only that we have been assured that Pélliot 'knows the ancient Chinese, Brahmi, Uigur, and Tibetan languages perfectly' (*Echo de Paris* of December 10); it is true that it was not he himself who said this, but he is doubtless too modest to do so.

However this may be, it certainly seems that early in his exploration Pélliot, like his Russian, English, German, and Japanese predecessors, was the only one to discover

> preserved by the sands of this desiccated country, the remains of an essentially Buddhist civilization that had flourished there during the first two centuries of the present era, and was abruptly destroyed around the year 1000 by Islam.

This is therefore not a relatively recent civilization 'where influences from India, Persia, Greece, and the Far East' mingled, and that simply came to be superimposed on earlier civilizations dating back many thousands of years. Now Chinese Turkestan is not far from Tibet; is Pélliot ignorant of the true age of Tibetan civilization, and does he believe it also to be 'essentially Buddhist' as many of his peers have claimed? The reality is that Buddhism never had anything but a completely superficial influence in these regions, and that in Tibet itself it would be difficult to find any traces of it, unfortunately for those who even now wish to make it the center of Buddhist religion. The ancient civilizations to which we have just alluded must thus have been buried under the sand, but to find them it would doubtless have been necessary to dig a bit deeper; it is truly regrettable that no one should have thought of this.

After spending some time at Urumachi, capital of Chinese Turkestan, Pélliot proceeded to Tuan Huang in Western Kan Su, knowing 'that about twenty kilometers from the city was a sizeable group of Buddhist caves called Ts'ien-Fo-Tong or Caves of the Thousand Buddhas.' Here again it is thus a Buddhist civilization that is involved; it would really seem that there were never any others in this country, or at least that this was the first to have left any vestiges, and nonetheless everything proves to us the contrary. One is obliged to think that there are things that, while very apparent to some, are completely invisible to others. 'We examined these Buddhist caves for a long while,' says Pélliot; 'there were almost five hundred dating from the sixth to the eleventh century, still covered with the paintings and inscriptions with which the donors decorated them.' Thus, at Tuan Huang as in Turkestan, there is nothing prior to the Christian era; all of this is almost modern, given that, on the admission of the sinologists themselves, 'a rigorously controlled chronology allows one to go as far back in Chinese history as four thousand years,' and these four thousand years are nothing when compared with the period, considered legendary, that preceded them.

But here is the most important discovery. At Urumachi, Pélliot heard that ancient manuscripts had been found a few years earlier in one of the caves at Tuan Huang.

> In 1900 a monk, who was clearing out one of the bigger caves, chanced upon a walled niche that, when opened, was found to be filled with manuscripts and paintings.

It is rather strange that all this remained in the same place from 1900 until 1908 without anyone being told that these manuscripts and paintings might be of some interest; even admitting that the monk was wholly illiterate, as Pélliot believes (which would be very surprising), he would nonetheless not have gone without announcing his find to people more capable of appreciating its value. But what is even more surprising is that this monk allowed strangers to examine these documents and to take away everything that they found interesting; never has any explorer encountered such compliance among Easterners, who generally guard everything that relates to the past and to the traditions of their country and their race with a jealous caution. We cannot cast doubt on Péllliot's account, however, but we have to think that not everyone attached the same importance to these documents as he, or they would long since have been safely stored in some monastery—let us call it Buddhist so as not to take from the sinologists all their illusions. No doubt, Pélliot was made to find these manuscripts just as curious travelers who visit Tibet are made to see many things so that they will be satisfied and not extend their investigations too far; it is both easier and more polite than to turn them away abruptly, and, as to politeness, the Chinese are known not to yield anything to any other people.

There was a bit of everything in this niche at Tuan Huang:

> texts in Brahmi, Tibetan, Uigur, but also many in Chinese; Buddhist, and Taoist manuscripts on paper or silk, a Nestorian Christian text, a Manichean fragment, works of history, geography, philosophy, literature, the archetypes of the classics [*sic*], the oldest prints in the Far East, sales records, leases, financial records, accounts, many paintings on silk, and finally, xylographs from the tenth and even the eighth centuries, the oldest in the world.

In this enumeration Taoist manuscripts seem to be found there as if by chance, just as the Nestorian and Manichean texts, of which the presence is rather surprising. On the other hand, since the xylograph was known in China long before the Christian era, it is hardly likely that the prints in question here are really 'the oldest in the world' as Pélliot believes. Pélliot, well pleased by his discovery, which he himself proclaims 'the most extraordinary that the history of the Far East has ever recorded,' hastened to return to China proper; the letters from Peking, which are too polite to permit any doubt as to the value of the documents he describes, beg him to send them photographs of the discoveries that would serve as the basis for a large publication.

Pélliot has now returned to France with his collection of paintings, bronzes, ceramics, and sculptures collected all along his route, and especially with manuscripts found at Kutchar and Tuan Huang. While admitting that these manuscripts have all the value some wish to attribute to them, we are left to wonder how the philologists are going to go about deciphering and translating them, and this task does not seem to be a very easy one.

Despite all the scholars' claims, the much vaunted progress of philology seems to be rather dubious judging by how oriental languages are still officially taught today. Concerning sinology in particular, people still follow the path of the first translators and little seems to have advanced in a half century. We can take the translations of Lao Tzu, for example, of which the first, by G. Pauthier, is surely the most deserving and conscientious, despite the inevitable imperfections. Even before it was published, this translation was violently criticized by Stanislaus Julien, who seems to have tried to deprecate it in favor of his own, which is nonetheless much inferior and only dates from 1842 while Pauthier's dates from 1833. In his introduction to the *Tao Te Ching*, moreover, Stanislaus Julien shares the views of the following statement by A. Rémusat in *Un Memoire sur Lao-tseu* which could still be repeated by modern sinologists.

> The text of the *Tao* is so full of obscurities, we have so few means to acquire a perfect understanding of it, so little knowledge of the circumstances to which the author alludes; in every respect we are so far from the ideas that influenced his writing, that it would be foolhardy to claim to discover exactly the meaning he had in mind.

Despite this admitted incomprehension, the translation of Stanislaus Julien (we shall see shortly what this is worth in itself) is still held to be authoritative and is the one to which official sinologists most readily turn.

In reality, leaving aside the very remarkable translation of the *I Ching* and its traditional commentaries by M. Philastre, a translation that is unfortunately very little understood by Western intellectuals, it must be recognized that nothing truly serious was done in this regard until the work of Matgioi. Before him, Chinese metaphysics was entirely unknown in Europe; one could even say wholly unsuspected without risking the accusation of exaggeration. Since the translations of the two books of the *Tao* and the *Te* by Matgioi have been seen and approved in the Far East by sages who retain the heritage of Taoist Science, which for us guarantees their perfect exactitude, Stanislaus Julien's translation must be compared to it. We shall be content to refer to the eloquent notes accompanying the tradition of *Tao* and *Te* published in *La Haute Science* (2nd year, 1894) in which Matgioi presents a number of mistranslations such as the following: 'It is good to place a shelf of jade in front of one and to mount a chariot of four horses,' instead of 'Joined together they go faster and more forcefully than a chariot of four horses.' We could cite at random a host of similar examples where a term signifying 'the blink of an eye' becomes 'a rhinoceros horn', or where money becomes 'a commoner' and its true value 'a wagon' and so forth; but here is something even more telling, that is, the appraisal of a native scholar reported in these words by Matgioi:

> Having in hand the French paraphrase by Julien, I then had the idea of re-translating it literally into common Chinese for the doctor who was teaching me. He first began to smile silently in the Eastern manner, then became indignant, and finally declared, 'The French must indeed be enemies of Asians if their scholars amuse themselves by knowingly distorting the works of Chinese philosophy and changing them into grotesque fabrications to be held up to the ridicule of the French masses.' I did not try to make my doctor believe that Julien imagined his to be a respectable translation, for he would then have questioned the worth of all our scholars. I preferred to let him doubt the sincerity of Julien alone; and thus it is that the latter has posthumously paid for the indiscretion he committed while living by tackling texts of which the meaning and import inevitably escaped him.

We think the example of Stanislaus Julien, who was a member of the Institute, gives a good idea of the value of philologists in general. Nonetheless there may be honorable exceptions and we even prefer to believe that Pélliot is one; it is now up to him to give us proof of it by accurately interpreting the texts he has brought back from his expedition. However this may be, as regards Taoist texts, today it should no longer be possible to demonstrate an ignorance of Chinese metaphysics that might have been excusable up to a point in the time of Rémusat and Stanislaus Julien, but that can no longer be so after the work of Matgioi, especially after the publication of his two most important works from this point of view, *La Voie Metaphysique* and *La Voie Rationelle.* But official scholars, always disdainful of anything that does not come from one of their own, are hardly capable of profiting from them precisely because of their peculiar mentality. This is a great pity for them, and if we are permitted to counsel Pélliot, we urge him with all our strength not to follow the unfortunate errors of his predecessors.

If we move from Chinese manuscripts to texts written in the languages of Central Asia or even in the sacred languages of India, we find ourselves in the presence of yet graver difficulties, for as we observed above, Pélliot himself recognizes that 'European philology has hardly begun to interpret these mysterious idioms.' We can go even further and say that among these languages, each of which has a script of its own, without counting the cryptographic systems very much still in use throughout the East, which in certain cases make deciphering completely impossible (even in Europe one finds inscriptions of this kind which have never been interpreted) among these languages, we say, there are a great number of which everything, even the name, is and will long remain unknown by Western scholars. In order to translate these texts they will probably turn to methods that the Egyptologists and Assyriologists have already used in other branches of philology; the interminable arguments that arise between them at every moment, their inability to agree on the most essential points of their science, as well as the obvious absurdities met with in all their interpretations, sufficiently illustrate the minimal value of the results they achieve, of which they are nonetheless so proud. The strangest thing is that these scholars claim to understand the languages they study even better than those who spoke and wrote them in the past; we do not exaggerate, for we have seen noted in manuscripts so-called interpolations which according to them prove that the copyist was mistaken about the meaning of the text he transcribed.

We are here far from the cautious reserve of the first sinologists mentioned above; yet if the claims of the philologists are always on the increase, their science is far from making a similarly rapid progress. Thus Egyptologists still use Champollion's method, their only fault being to apply it solely to inscriptions from the Greek and

Roman periods when Egyptian writing had become purely phonetic following the degeneration of the language, whereas earlier it had been hieroglyphic, that is to say ideographic like Chinese writing. Moreover, the failing of all official philologists is to want to interpret sacred languages, nearly all of which are ideographic, as they do common languages, which are merely alphabetic or phonetic. Let us add that there are languages that combine the ideographic and alphabetic systems; biblical Hebrew is like this, as Fabre d'Olivet has shown in *The Hebraic Tongue Restored*; and we can note in passing that this is sufficient to make it clear that the true meaning of the Bible has nothing in common with the ridiculous interpretations that have been attributed to it from the commentaries of Protestant as well as Catholic theologians—which moreover are based on versions that are entirely erroneous—to the critiques of modern exegetes who are still at the point of asking how it happens that in Genesis there are passages where God is called אלהים and others where He is called יהוה, without seeing that these two terms, the first of which is a plural, have a completely different meaning and that in reality neither has ever designated God.

Furthermore, what makes the translation of ideographic languages almost impossible is the multitude of meanings belonging to the hierogrammatical characters, each of which corresponds to a different if analogous idea according as it is related to one level or another of the universe; from this it follows that three principal meanings can always be distinguished, which are in turn subdivided into a great number of secondary and more particular significations. This explains why one cannot properly speaking translate the sacred books; one can only make a paraphrase or a commentary, and this is what the philologists and exegetes ought to resign themselves to, if only they could grasp the most outward meaning; unfortunately, up to now they do not seem to have attained even this modest result. Let us hope that Pélliot will be more fortunate than his colleagues, and that the manuscripts he possesses will not remain for him a dead letter, and let us wish him all courage in the arduous task he has undertaken.

8

PROFANE SCIENCE IN LIGHT OF TRADITIONAL DOCTRINES

ALTHOUGH we have often explained what ought to be the normal attitude toward profane science on the part of anyone who represents or merely expounds a traditional doctrine of any sort, it seems from certain remarks that have recently come to us from various quarters, that everyone has not yet fully understood it. We must admit that there is an excuse for this: the attitude in question is difficult to conceive for those who have been affected to some degree by the modern mentality, which is to say for the immense majority of our contemporaries, at least in the West. Rare are those who succeed in fully disencumbering themselves of the prejudices inherent in this mentality, and which have been imposed on them by their education and by the very ambiance in which they live. Now, among these prejudices one of the strongest is certainly a belief in the value of modern science, which is really the same thing as profane science, and as a result many have a more or less unconscious desire not to admit that the real or supposed results of this science are something that can be disregarded.

First of all we will recall that in every order it is the profane point of view as such that is illegitimate, and this point of view consists essentially in considering things without a link to any transcendent principle and as if they were independent of every principle, which it ignores purely and simply, even when it does not go as far as to deny them outright. This definition applies equally to the domain of action and to that of knowledge; in the latter it is evident that such is the case of modern science in its entirety, and that as a consequence modern science has no right to be considered as true knowledge since, even if it should happen to state things that are true, its manner of presenting them is nonetheless illegitimate, and it is in any case unable to give the reason for their truth which can only lie in their dependence on principles. Of course, when we speak of knowledge this does not concern the practical applications that can result from this science, for these applications are completely independent of the value of the science as such and consequently do not interest us here. Besides, scientists themselves readily recognize that they make use of forces the nature of which is completely unknown to them. This ignorance no doubt accounts for much of the danger that these applications too often present, but this is another question which we do not have to pursue at present.

It could be asked whether, in spite of everything, such a science might not be legitimized by re-establishing, for the part of truth it can contain of a relative order, the link with principles which alone would permit this truth to be effectively understood as such. Certainly this is not impossible in some cases, but then it would not really be a question of the same science, since this would imply a complete change of point of view, and a traditional point of view would thereby be substituted for the profane point of view; and it must not be forgotten that a science is not defined solely by its object but also by the point of view from which it considers the object. If it were to happen, what could be preserved would have to be most carefully distinguished from what on the contrary would have to be eliminated, that is to say all the false ideas which ignorance of principles has only too easily allowed to be introduced; and the very formulation of truths would most often have to be corrected, for it is almost always seriously influenced by the false ideas with which the truths in question are associated in profane science. We ourselves, in one of our works, have given some evidence of this in regard to certain aspects of modern mathematics;[1] and let no one come and say that in such an instance the correction of terminology would have but little fundamental importance, or even that

1. See *The Metaphysical Principles of the Infinitesimal Calculus.*

it would not merit the effort required, under the pretext that mathematicians are not themselves dupes of the absurdities implied in the language they use. First of all, incorrect language always presupposes some confusion in thought, and it is more serious than might be thought to refuse to correct this error, and to treat it as something negligible or indifferent. Next, even if professional mathematicians finally realize the falsehood of certain ideas, nonetheless, by continuing to speak in ways that reflect these same false ideas, they contribute to spreading or maintaining them among those who in any measure receive their teaching, directly or indirectly, and who cannot examine things as closely as they. Finally, and most importantly, the fact of using terminology to which no plausible significance is attached is nothing but another manifestation of the growing tendency of modern science to become nothing more than an empty 'conventionalism', a tendency that is itself characteristic of the phase of 'dissolution' succeeding that of 'solidification' in the last periods of the cycle.[2] It would be truly curious and moreover very worthy of an age of intellectual disorder like ours, if, in wanting to prove that the objections we have formulated against their science were not really applicable to them, people were to advance precisely an argument that on the contrary only provided a still more ample confirmation of it!

This leads us directly to a more general consideration: we know that people sometimes reproach us for raising an argument against modern scientific theories that are hardly accepted any longer by scientists themselves, or concerning which they at least have reservations not held by their predecessors. To take an example, it is true that transformism has lost much ground in 'scientific' circles without it being possible to go so far as to say that it has no more advocates, which would be a manifest exaggeration. But it is no less true that it continues to spread as before, and with the same 'dogmatic' assurance, in textbooks and in works of popularization, that is to say in all that is in fact accessible to those who are not 'specialists', so much so that as regards the influence it exercises on the general mentality nothing has truly changed, and in this respect it still

2. See *The Reign of Quantity and the Signs of the Times*.

retains the same 'currency'. Moreover, it must be well understood that the importance we attach to this fact, which can also be noted for other 'out of date' or 'outgrown' theories (according to the fashionable expressions), is in no way due to any particular interest we bear toward the 'general public'. The true reason is that these theories affect without distinction all those who, as we just said, are not 'specialists', among whom there are surely some, however few they may be, who, if not subjected to such influences, would possess possibilities of comprehension that, on the contrary, would hardly be expected among scientists irremediably enclosed in their 'specialties'. In truth, although for their part many of these scientists have renounced the gross forms of transformism, we are not sure that it is not simply in order to replace them with ideas which, even if more subtle, are worth no more fundamentally and are perhaps even more dangerous. In any case, why do they maintain a blameworthy equivocation, continuing to speak of 'evolution' as they always have, if what they now really mean by this term hardly has any connection with what used to be designated by it? Must one see here, as well, one of the manifestations of current scientific 'conventionalism', or simply an example of the tendency that words have today, even in everyday usage, to completely lose their normal meanings? However this may be, what is rather strange is that while certain people reproach us for not sufficiently taking into consideration what could be called scientific 'topicality', in other circles there are people who, on the contrary, certainly do not forgive us for thinking and saying that materialism is no longer the only danger there is reason to decry, nor even the principal or most formidable one. It is very difficult to satisfy everyone, and we must add, moreover, that for our part this is something that has never greatly preoccupied us.

Let us now return to the question of the legitimation of the modern sciences. If, as we said, this legitimation is possible for some, it is not so for all equally, for it is a necessary condition that a science have an object that is legitimate in itself even if, because of its profane character, its manner of considering it is not legitimate. Now this condition is not fulfilled by those sciences—we ought rather to say so-called sciences—which are really only specific products of the modern deviation. A typical case of this sort is psychoanalysis, and there is no good reason to attempt to link to higher principles what is properly only an aberration due to the action of the lowest psychic influences; one might as well try to legitimize spiritism or 'surrealist' divagations, which have a wholly similar origin, the only difference being that these latter are not admitted into the categories of 'official' teaching. On the other hand, as regards those modern sciences that have at least a legitimate object, it must not be forgotten that for many of them one has to take into account their 'residual' character regarding certain ancient sciences, as we have explained on other occasions, so that legitimizing them would amount to a more or less integral restoration of the traditional sciences to which they correspond and of which they are only the degenerate vestiges resulting from the forgetting of principles. But this restoration itself would not be without difficulty, for among these traditional sciences are some, like astrology, the true 'keys' to which seem to have been lost completely, and great care would have to be taken not to confuse them with more or less recent deformations that one meets with today under the same name and which themselves are very much affected by the profane point of view that more and more encroaches on everything.

The question we have just been considering has as yet only a 'theoretical' interest, as it were, for in fact the legitimation in question has not yet been undertaken in any case, so that when it is a question of modern science one is solely in the presence of profane science. With respect to traditional doctrines this can only be considered to be purely and simply non-existent; in other words, there is no need to preoccupy oneself with knowing whether it agrees or disagrees with these doctrines, with which, because of its lack of principles, it could have no effective link. If there is disagreement one can be certain that the error is necessarily on the part of the profane science, for traditional data cannot be the object of any doubt for anyone who understands their true nature. If on the contrary there is agreement, this is all the better for the science in question, but only for it, for this shows that it has managed to arrive, albeit by very roundabout and uncertain ways, at the truth about certain particular points. This concurrence, which has only a wholly accidental character, is of no importance to traditional doctrines, for these have no need of any outward 'confirmation'. Moreover, it would be a strange kind of confirmation made by appeals to a science for which the truths in question, as all of its theories, can never be anything except mere, more or less probable, hypotheses. For the same reasons there is no additional reason to try to associate traditional data with ideas borrowed from profane science or more or less directly inspired by it; this is a perfectly vain undertaking which could only be the work of people like the occultists, for example, who are completely ignorant of the true import of the fragmentary elements they have taken from the little they know of different traditions. We have often enough explained the inanity of this sort of 'syncretistic' and hybrid construction for it to be unnecessary for us to enlarge on it again.

Furthermore, we have also had occasion to point out the weakness, not to say more, of the attitude customarily called 'apologetic', which consists in trying to defend a tradition against attacks such as those by modern science, by disputing these arguments on their own ground, something that almost always entails unfortunate concessions and that in any case implies a misunderstanding of the transcendent character of traditional doctrine. This is the usual attitude of exoterists, and it may be thought that very often they are especially driven by the fear that numerous adherents of their tradition will be led astray by scientific objections, or what are so called, raised against it; but beside the fact that this 'quantitative' consideration is itself of a rather profane order, these objections merit all the less having such importance attached to them since the science that inspires them changes continually—and this should suffice to prove what little soundness they have. When one sees theologians, for example, preoccupied with 'making the Bible agree with science', it is only too easy to see how illusory is such work, since it constantly has to be redone as scientific theories change, this without counting the drawback of appearing to link tradition to the present state of profane science, that is, to theories that in a few years will perhaps no longer be accepted by anyone, if they have not already been abandoned by scientists—for this also can happen, as the objections that are challenged are more usually the work of popularizers than of the scientists themselves. Instead of clumsily reducing sacred scriptures to such a level, these theologians would surely do much better to penetrate their true meaning as far as possible and to expound them purely and simply for the benefit of those who are able to understand and who, if they understood them effectively, would thereby no longer be tempted to let themselves be influenced by the hypotheses of profane science, any more than by the dissolving 'critique' of a modernist and rationalist, that is, essentially anti-traditional, exegesis, the alleged results of which no longer need to be taken into consideration by those who are conscious of what tradition really is. Whoever expounds a traditional doctrine, exoteric as well as esoteric, not only has the strictest right but even the duty to refrain from the least compromise with the profane point of view, whatever the domain in question. But in the West today, where are those who still understand that this must be so? Perhaps some will say that, after all, this is the business of theologians (since we have just taken them as an example) and not our own. But we are not among those who think one can dissociate oneself from attacks upon any tradition and who are even always ready to congratulate themselves on attacks aimed at a tradition other than their own, as if these were blows against 'rivals', and as if ultimately these attacks did not always affect the traditional spirit itself. The type of 'apologetics' we have discussed shows only too well to what degree these attacks have succeeded in weakening the traditional spirit even among those who believe themselves its defenders.

Now there is still a point that we must clarify in order to avoid any misunderstanding. It certainly must not be thought that anyone who intends to keep a rigorously traditional attitude must thenceforth be forbidden to speak about the theories of profane science. On the contrary, when there is reason, he can and must denounce their errors and dangers, and this especially when he finds in them assertions clearly running counter to the data of tradition. But he must do so in a way that never constitutes a discussion 'between equals', which is only possible on the condition that one place oneself on profane ground. Indeed, what is really at issue is a judgment made in the name of a higher authority, that of traditional doctrine, for of course it is this doctrine alone that counts here, while the individualities who express it have not the slightest importance in themselves. Now as far as we know no one has ever dared claim that a judgment could be assimilated to a discussion or to 'polemics'. If because of a prejudice due to incomprehension, the bad faith of which is unhappily not always absent, those who misunderstand the authority of tradition claim to see 'polemics' where there is no shadow of it, there is obviously no way to prevent them from doing so, any more than one can prevent an ignorant person or a fool from taking traditional doctrines for 'philosophy', but this is not worth the least attention. At least all those who understand what tradition is and whose opinion alone counts will know perfectly well what to think; as for us, if there are profane people who would like to engage us in discussion, we shall warn them once for all that, since we will never consent to descend to their level nor to place ourselves at their point of view, their efforts will always fall into the void.

LIST OF ORIGINAL SOURCES

V.I. = *Le Voile d'Isis*, *E. T.* = *Études Traditionnelles*

PART ONE

1. *La Gnose* Nov. 1909
2. *E. T.* Oct.–Nov. 1946
3. *E. T.* July–Aug. 1947
4. *E. T.* Sept. 1947
5. *E. T.* March 1949
6. *El-Ma'rifah* May 1931
7. *La Gnose* June–July–Aug. 1910

PART TWO

1. *V.I.* April 1934
2. *La Gnose* April–May 1910
3. *V.I.* April 1935
4. *La Gnose* Jan. 1912

PART THREE

1. *E. T.* July 1934
2. *E. T.* May 1940
3. *E. T.* June 1940
4. *E. T.* Dec. 1937
5. *E. T.* 1940
6. *La Gnose* Dec. 1909 and *La Gnose* Aug.–Nov. 1911
7. *La Gnose* Jan. 1910
8. *E. T.* April–May 1950

INDEX

Printed in the United States
113730LV00002B/251/A

9 780900 588556